Dedicated to assholes everywhere.

Especially you.

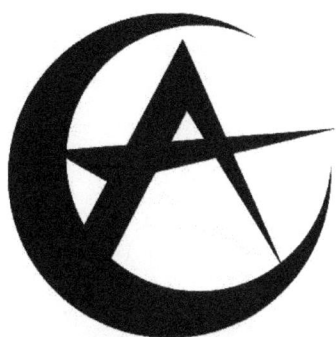

ASSHOLE™
ZODIAC

Todd and Karen Hayes

Asshole Zodiac™

First Edition Paperback

Table of Contents

Preface 1

The 12 Asshole Personalities 3

    The Scheming Asshole 5

    The Sanctimonious Asshole 13

    The Boastful Asshole 21

    The Cynical Asshole 29

    The Analytical Asshole 37

    The Dramatic Asshole 45

    The Martyr Asshole 53

    The Stoic Asshole 61

    The Codependent Asshole...69

    The Jester Asshole 77

    The Bureaucratic Asshole...85

    The Vanishing Asshole...93

Appendix A: The Quiz 99

Appendix B: Motivational Drivers 110

Appendix C: Secondary Profiles 114

Appendix D: Notes about your asshole friends 115

General Disclaimer: The publisher is not liable for any of the assholes featured in or contributing to this book. The Asshole Zodiac is a satirical personality framework intended for entertainment, self-reflection, and for navigating the jerks in your life. Any resemblance to real persons, living or delusional, is purely coincidental — unless, of course, you recognize yourself in a profile and it makes you laugh or changes your life forever in a positive way.

Disclaimers by Asshole Type:

For Sanctimonious, Boastful, or Bureaucratic Assholes: This content is not intended to diagnose, defame, or legally implicate anyone (even if a quiz result or a behavioral description screams out from the pages to trigger you). All descriptions are exaggerated archetypes and should be taken as seriously as a wine horoscope. If you are offended or plotting litigation, please consult your therapist, a Stoic Asshole, or literally *anyone* with a sense of humor before emailing our legal team.

For Scheming Assholes: No one here is trying to outmaneuver you. We know we'd lose. You're safe.

For Cynical and Analytical Assholes: Feel free to submit condescending retorts and criticisms using memes and detailed spreadsheets. We will not likely read them.

For Codependent and Martyr Assholes: These profiles are not intended to hurt your feelings. It's all in good fun. You are the salt of the earth, and we love you for being exactly who you are and for everything you do.

For Stoic, Scheming, and Vanishing Assholes: You have more important things to think about than finishing this book. Don't worry about it. Godspeed.

For Dramatic, Jester, Vanishing, Cynical, and Boastful Assholes: We absolutely do not advise you to drink large quantities of alcohol or smoke or snort anything just because it might fit your proposed asshole profile. Take a break. Drink some green tea instead. Call your mother.

Preface

Healing the World, One Asshole at a Time

"Everyone is an asshole," Karen said. "You just have to figure out what type of asshole they are."

We were two cocktails into our date and the conversation was riveting. How many misunderstandings could be avoided by simply identifying a particular asshole type and aligning behaviors in context with someone's underlying motivations?

The night was full of belly laughs, and problem solving, and pee breaks. This was a poster-child moment of why people drink on dates. Unlike most alcohol-assisted dialogues, however, this idea still felt worthy of investigation on the following day.

Thus began our journey to creating a comprehensive framework for profiling assholes for the benefit of mankind. Needless to say, I didn't wait long to propose marriage to this brilliant woman.

Traditional Eastern and Western zodiac frameworks focus on defining the characteristics that you were born with. Asshole Zodiac profiles are more about how you've learned to define and navigate the world after being born. This begins with your primary motivational driver, which is detailed in **Appendix B**.

If you wish, you can start with the quiz in **Appendix A** and score your own asshole profile. You can also take the quiz online at **https://www.assholezodiac.com**. Most people have a primary and secondary asshole type, which may switch positions depending on your mood or depending on the assholes you're hanging with at the time you take the quiz. Retake the quiz as often as you need, but do try to answer the questions honestly according to what you know is your nature, as opposed to answering as the person you want to be.

Each chapter of Asshole Zodiac includes a personality profile with their aptitudes, tell-tale phrases, relationship dynamics, best love matches*, and life journeys. While you may share a profile with a person or fictional character mentioned, that doesn't mean you share the same opinions, habits, or tactics, only that your motivational drivers and triggers will be very similar and even predictable. No asshole is better than another. We all have noble roles to play and paths to walk.

In these pages, we hope you will gain insights about yourself and the people you're with every day to help reduce frustrations and promote understanding. If you know what type of asshole you're dealing with at any given moment, the element of surprise is no longer a factor when trying compute a response to them. It's just harder to be offended by anything they say when you understand their profile. Even better, it can arm you with the right approach to avoid conflict, offer strategic motivations, and improve many relationships that never needed to be contentious in the first place.

This project started as a joke. It's evolved into a Rosetta Stone of personality type meaning, motivations, and tendencies that has plenty of practical applications. It also provides a starting point for the acceptance required to heal relationships and lighten moods. Start by accepting your own asshole profile and you'll know what I mean.

Happy spelunking,

Todd

*Note: The best love match sections may sometimes seem asymmetrical between chapters. It's because what's best for the featured personality type may not be perfect for their matched personality. That doesn't mean the matches represented are one-sided relationships, which is unfortunately more common than not in the dating world. These are good matches.

The 12 Asshole Personalities

"You can forgive someone and still think they are an asshole.
Forgiveness doesn't change what a person is, it only changes you."
— Shannon L. Alder

Give me six lines written by the hand of the most honest man,
and I will find something in them which will hang him."

— Cardinal Richelieu

The Scheming Asshole

Animal Spirit: Octopus

Motivational Driver: Moral Enforcement

Best Traits: Visionary, calculated

Worst Traits: Manipulative, two-faced

Scheming Asshole Profile

You were born to lead with vision, confidence, and an uncanny ability to get others on board. A master of perception and planning, you're always five steps ahead, effortlessly guiding the game without needing the spotlight (if you want recognition you'll plan for it).

Your ambition is magnetic, and your presence commands attention. Some may misread your strategic mind as manipulative, but really you just know how to influence outcomes. You thrive in high-pressure environments and are never rattled when others crumble. Your strength is your mind; your gift is knowing how to make people move without them realizing they were moved. You're the architect of your reality and everyone else's. When you walk into a room, people know something important is happening. You're the puppet master the world needs to stay in motion, fearless, focused, and just a little dangerous. You are the empire builder of the personalities.

Famous Scheming Assholes

The Puppet Masters: Visionary, manipulative, and five steps ahead

- Steve Jobs
- Kris Jenner
- Bill Clinton
- Margaret Thatcher
- Rob Mariano
- Niccolò Machiavelli

Career Aptitude for Scheming Assholes

Political Strategist or Campaign Manager: manipulates outcomes with purpose

Corporate Executive or C-Suite Fixer: long-game visionary in high-stakes leadership

Creative Director or Brand Architect: controls perception behind the scenes

Scheming Asshole Archetypes in Literature and Film

Frank Underwood in *House of Cards*

Tom Ripley in *The Talented Mr. Ripley*

Vito Corleone in *The Godfather*

Lady Macbeth in *The Tragedy of Macbeth*

Best Entertainment for Scheming Assholes

Games: Strategy games (chess, poker, capture the flag)

Music: Industrial and Dark Trip-Hop (e.g., Massive Attack, Nine Inch Nails)

Stories: Spy thrillers, political dramas, documentaries on manipulation or con artists

Exercise/sports: Fencing, Chess Boxing, Martial Arts (tactically stimulating competitions that benefit from preplanned moves)

Other Activities: Escape rooms, Reddit rabbit holes

Cocktail, Beer, and Wine Pairings for Scheming Assholes

Cocktail: Negroni — bitter, refined, complex, and always a power move. A Negroni is a drink that lets others think they're keeping up.

Beer: Belgian Tripel — strong, elegant, and deceptive

Wine: Bordeaux Blend — strategic, layered, built to dominate

Tips for Dealing with a Scheming Asshole

Working Relationships: Approach with quiet competence. Don't posture or overshare. They'll test your motives like a cold-war spy. Show them how your success benefits them and leave your ego at the door.

Domestic Relationships: Trust is earned in layers. Be consistent and emotionally intelligent. If they sense you're manipulating them, they'll outmaneuver you and pretend it was your idea all along.

Scheming Asshole Phrases

An easy way to identify a Scheming Asshole (other than having them take the quiz, which is the easiest) is when you hear them utter a phrase that reveals their intent. It is likely that someone saying one of these phrases has the Scheming trait in their profile as either their primary or secondary personality.

I knew this might happen. I have a workaround. The Schemer is five steps ahead and anticipates bending the rules to suit their moral calculus. They probably won't tell you about their plans unless they need to.

Note: a Stoic Asshole may also say something like this, but their motivation for making alternate plans is to protect their psyche rather than advancing a scheme.

Technically, I didn't lie. The Schemer is not above weaponizing semantics to maintain the illusion of integrity while doing exactly what they want to. And their argument will probably hold up in court.

It's not manipulation if it serves the greater good. The Schemer is an expert at rationalizing tactics, confident that their intelligence and/or ethics is superior to the pedestrians they've outwitted.

Triggers for Scheming Assholes

The Octopus has emotional and situational triggers that can make them lose their composure, at least momentarily. The table below lists some common triggers and some ideas on how to calm their nerves during and after a triggering.

Trigger	Why it upsets them	How to ease their nerves
Being outmaneuvered in public	If someone calls their bluff, exposes their plan, or beats them at the game they've designed	Acknowledge their insight privately and let them regain their footing
Being morally challenged	If someone implies they are unethical or selfish, it threatens their carefully crafted identity	Frame critiques as mutual ethical refinements, not as an accusation
Chaotic or illogical systems	If they're dropped into a disorganized, dysfunctional, or overly emotional environment, they will become anxious	Ask for their ideas on fixing the system or for making it more predictable

Trigger	Why it upsets them	How to ease their nerves
Lack of access to power brokers	If they're sidelined, excluded from decision-making circles, or forced to follow someone else's inferior plan, expect strategic withdrawal or even subtle sabotage to turn things around	Bring them in for advice to restore their sense of control
Blatant emotional displays	Raw vulnerability, especially in strategic opponents, makes them uncomfortable whenever it derails their plans or makes them feel exposed by contrast	Reassure them calmly with logic and the intent to reestablish order

Love for Scheming Assholes

Best Love Match: Analytical Asshole

Why it works: A master strategist needs a truth-teller who sees through the BS. Analytical keeps Scheming grounded; Scheming gives Analytical purpose and power. It's a ruthless and brilliant merger of mastermind and logic.

Bonus Love Sparks: Power couple vibes, silent mind-melds, strategic pillow talk.

Scheming Asshole Relationship Dynamics

The table below lists potential collaborations and pitfalls for the Scheming Asshole as they deal with each of the other assholes in the zodiac.

Assholes	Relationship Dynamic	Areas of Risk	Bonding Opportunities
Sanctimonious Asshole (Owl)	Mutual distrust masked as respect	Power struggle over who knows best	Aligning on a shared enemy or a high-minded goal
Boastful Asshole (Peacock)	Octopus manipulates as Peacock performs	Peacock overshares; Schemer uses it	Strategic image-building — one pulls strings, one shines
Cynical Asshole (Cat)	Wary allies with dry banter	Paralysis by overthinking, mutual distrust	Snarky intelligence, shared loathing of obvious people

Assholes	Relationship Dynamic	Areas of Risk	Bonding Opportunities
Analytical Asshole (Falcon)	Respectful collaborators (when goals align)	Emotional cold wars, perfectionist clashes	Logic-driven planning sessions, mutual love of strategy
Dramatic Asshole (Cockatoo)	Schemer finds them exhausting	Cockatoo overshares, Octopus emotionally checks out	Chaos plus control = effective (but volatile) drama team
Martyr Asshole (Elephant)	Schemer exploits, Martyr enables	Resentment ensues when Martyr catches on	Saving each other via mission-based manipulation
Stoic Asshole (Tortoise)	Quiet power pairing	Passive-aggressive stalemates	Strategic silence, loyalty built over time
Codependent Asshole (Retriever)	Emotional sponge for Schemer's games	Retriever becomes drained and dependent	One gives devotion while the other gives direction
Jester Asshole (Chimpanzee)	A balancing act of chaos and control	Schemer sees Jester as unpredictable and unserious	Jester provides cover for Octopus' schemes; occasional mischief duo
Bureaucratic Asshole (Beaver)	Procedural tension: one bends rules, one enforces	Friction when Schemer shortcuts a process	Combining backdoor access (Octopus) with front-door logic (Beaver)
Vanishing Asshole (Fox)	Unspoken irritations, no closure	Zero communication; suspicion builds	Subtle respect for each other's emotional evasiveness

Ideal Purpose and Life Journey for The Scheming Asshole

The ultimate life purpose for a Scheming Asshole is to learn to wield power responsibly using their gifts of strategy and foresight. Not for domination, but for guiding systems and souls toward a purposeful order.

Along the way they will gain momentum and insight by mentoring emerging leaders, creating long-term plans (vision boards, roadmaps), and researching biographical information about historical masterminds that they admire.

Their successful journey begins with experimental manipulations of those around them, learning their limits and the limits of others, and learning which rules can be bent to speed them to their goals. It ends as a transformative architect that combines influence and integrity in building something brilliant for the betterment of society (or at least for those they care about the most).

I am not free while any woman is unfree, even when
her shackles are very different from my own."

— Audre Lorde

The Sanctimonious Asshole

Animal Spirit: Owl

Motivational Driver: Moral Enforcement

Best Traits: Disciplined, principled

Worst Traits: Judgy, passive-aggressive

Sanctimonious Asshole Profile

You are the ethical lighthouse in the fog, unwavering, principled, and deeply committed to doing what's right, even when no one is watching (although the miscreants are always watching).

You are unapologetically exacting. You hold yourself and others to a high standard out of a sincere belief that we can all be better. You're the moral anchor in your group, the one who sees injustice and speaks out. Some might call you intense, but that's just because you actually care. Your dedication to values makes you a trustworthy leader and an inspiring friend. You hold power not through force, but through integrity. People come to you for truth — and you never let them down. Your energy uplifts the righteous and humbles the careless. You don't just walk-the-walk, you insist the path be properly paved. You are the gold standard in a messy world of shortcuts and that makes people notice.

Famous Sanctimonious Assholes

The Holy Judge: Well-disciplined and morally rigid

- Al Gore
- Elizabeth Warren
- Immanuel Kant
- Cotton Mather
- Judge Judy

Career Aptitude for Sanctimonious Assholes

Ethics Officer / Compliance Director: enforces moral frameworks

Judge or Public Defender: righteous leadership through law

Nonprofit Leader: crusades for systemic improvement

Sanctimonious Asshole Archetypes in Literature and Film

Inspector Javert in *Les Misérables*

Atticus Finch in *To Kill a Mockingbird*

Galadriel in *The Lord of the Rings*

Ned Flanders in *The Simpsons*

Steve Rogers in *Marvel Cinematic Universe*

Best Entertainment for Sanctimonious Assholes

Games: Empire building games and strategy games that include finding a betrayer/spy (like Among Us)

Music: Classical music and choral arrangements

Stories: True crime, historical dramas, morality plays, documentaries with a social cause, TED Talks

Exercise/sports: Marathons, martial arts, or yoga

Other Activities: Ethical debates and church volunteering (they may also become obsessed with reality tv shows where people have hidden agendas, but they watch because of an addiction to being offended)

Cocktails, Beer, and Wine Pairings for Sanctimonious Assholes

Cocktail: Classic Old Fashioned — timeless, no-nonsense, righteous. This cocktail doesn't chase trends; it is the standard.

Beer: Trappist Ale — brewed by monks, moral as hell

Wine: Old World Chardonnay — restrained, serious, judgmental

Sanctimonious Asshole Phrases

An easy way to identify a Sanctimonious Asshole (other than having them take the quiz, which is the easiest) is when you hear them utter a phrase that reveals their intent. It is likely that someone saying one of these phrases has the Sanctimonious trait in their profile as either their primary or secondary personality.

It's not about me. It's about what's right. It's definitely about them, but by wrapping their argument in ethics, a challenge to their opinion now appears aggressive and problematic.

I don't understand how anyone with a conscience could think otherwise. The Owl's viewpoint is not only correct, it is morally mandatory. Further dissent reveals a character flaw.

Well, some of us still care about integrity. Translation: I'm disappointed in you, but I'll pretend this just a sad truth instead of me giving you a smug jab.

Triggers for Sanctimonious Assholes

The Owl has emotional and situational triggers that can make them lose their composure, at least momentarily. The table below lists some common triggers and some ideas on how to calm their nerves during and after a triggering.

Trigger	Why it upsets them	How to ease their nerves
Being morally questioned	A surprise interrogation on ethics may challenge their belief in their own moral authority	Listen to and acknowledge their values before offering alternative views to make it a discourse
Being disrespected or dismissed	Being dismissive of their opinion undermines their identity as a moral compass for the masses	Show deference to their principles, even if you disagree; Follow a dismissive comment with, "actually I do respect your position"
Rule breaking	Blatant rule breaking feels like an attack on order or authority	Pose the argument for rule breaking based on a principled solution
Being outvoted or overruled	Being overruled on a sensitive subject threatens the Owl's ethical leadership amongst their peers	Reframe the opposing decision around values instead of implying they are wrong
Mockery of serious issues	Purposeful disrespect is a trigger, especially if the issue is dear to their heart	Validate the seriousness of the issue before shifting tone and casting shade

Love for Sanctimonious Assholes

Best Match: Martyr Asshole

Why it works: Both assholes value loyalty, integrity, and service. Sanctimonious provides vision and standards while Martyr brings work ethic and emotional endurance. Together, they build righteous empires and judge others from the moral high ground.

Bonus Love Spark: Sunday mornings full of lists, service projects, and shared indignation

Tips for Dealing with a Sanctimonious Asshole

Working Relationships: Frame your contributions as being for the greater good. Lead with ethics and logic. They'll respect competence but demand moral consistency.

Domestic Relationships: They need to feel morally aligned with you. Validate their values, even if you disagree. Don't mock their seriousness — it's how they feel safe.

Sanctimonious Asshole Relationship Dynamics

The table below lists potential collaborations and pitfalls for the Sanctimonious Asshole as they deal with each of the other assholes in the zodiac.

Assholes	Relationship Dynamic	Areas of Risk	Bonding Opportunities
Boastful Asshole (Peacock)	Owl judges as Peacock preens	Owl sees Peacock as shallow	Possible shared stage with one moralizing and one glamorizing
Cynical Asshole (Cat)	Philosophical tension	Owl feels undermined by Cat's sarcasm	Mutual critique of societal flaws
Analytical Asshole (Falcon)	Logic meets ethics	Both can turn cold/ unyielding	Data-driven morality projects are a win
Dramatic Asshole (Cockatoo)	Oil and holy water	Owl wary of the Cockatoo chaos	Passion for causes when aligned
Martyr Asshole (Elephant)	Ideal partners in guilt	Co-misery spiral	Saving the world together

Assholes	Relationship Dynamic	Areas of Risk	Bonding Opportunities
Stoic Asshole (Tortoise)	Keeps a respectful distance	Mutual emotional repression	Quiet rituals, honor systems, and shared societal disappointments
Codependent Asshole (Golden Retriever)	Owl leads, Codependent follows	Retriever can lose their identity	Devotion to moral service or shared values
Jester Asshole (Chimpanzee)	Moral police vs. class clown	Owl shames and Jester rebels	Potential for comedy with a conscience
Bureaucratic Asshole (Beaver)	Policy twins	Risk of rigidity overload	Shared love of order and fairness
Vanishing Asshole (Fox)	Owl demands accountability and Fox vanishes	Constant tension	Possible allies in exposing corruption
Scheming Asshole (Octopus)	Complicated chess match	Owl hides motives while Owl demands transparency	Alignment in righteous manipulation

Ideal Purpose and Life Journey for The Sanctimonious Asshole

The ultimate life purpose for a Sanctimonious Asshole is to use their gifts of wisdom and ethical clarity to transform into a morally just leader who is well balanced by humility and worldly knowledge.

Along the way they will gain momentum by experiencing moral gray areas, including exposure to different cultures, religions, and ideologies that expand their consciousness. They begin to preach less and listen more. They start to appreciate values, motivations, and rationales that were previously invisible to them, softening their heart to be more inclusive and less triggered by opposing viewpoints.

A successful journey begins with their affinity for self-righteous behavior, which leads to rejection or distancing by less morally rigid personalities. Instead of turning bitter and reclusive, they go through a period of observation and self-reflection to redefine what is most important in life. In the end, they serve as a peaceful lighthouse for those who need it most, free from the weight of their own judgy instincts, easily scaling truth, empathy, and compassion, and leading others by example.

"I've never been interested in being invisible."

— Megan Thee Stallion

The Boastful Asshole

Animal Spirit: Peacock

Motivational Driver: Performance

Best Traits: Ambitious, polished

Worst Traits: Needy, arrogant

Boastful Asshole Profile

Charming, magnetic, and driven, you're the star that all others orbit. You have a natural flair for attention and an enviable work ethic to match. People might say you're self-obsessed, but they're just noticing how much time you've invested in becoming your best self.

Confidence is your currency. You spend it freely to show those watching how easy it is to be fabulous. Your ambition is unmatched, and your sensitivity only makes you more relatable. You see life as a stage, and you perform with flair, charisma, and vulnerability. You are quick to celebrate wins (especially your own), but that doesn't slow you down. That pride and work ethic comes from a deep desire to matter.

You inspire others to dream bigger and dress better. In your world, there's always a spotlight and you sometimes generously let others bask in its glow. You are a walking motivational poster with a perfect smile.

Famous Boastful Assholes

The Spotlight Addict: ambitious, charming, needs praise

- Muhammad Ali

- Tom Cruise

- Megan Thee Stallion

- Kim Kardashian

- Lizzo

Career Aptitude for Boastful Assholes

Public Relations / Spokesperson: thrives in the spotlight

Entertainer / Influencer: using that stage presence to inform and delight

Entrepreneur / CEO: builds empires with flair

Luxury Brand Sales / Fashion Designer: high-stakes image and ambition

Boastful Asshole Archetypes in Literature and Film

Tony Stark in *Iron Man*

Jordan Belfort in *The Wolf of Wall Street*

Regina George in *Mean Girls*

Ed Bloom, Sr. in *Big Fish*

Gilderoy Lockhart in *Harry Potter and the Chamber of Secrets*

Best Entertainment for Boastful Assholes

Games: Charades, Pictionary, Streetfighter, Jackbox Games, Just Dance, Call of Duty, Fortnite

Music: Pop-Power Anthems or Glam Rock (like *Bohemian Rhapsody*)

Stories: Biopics, redemptive musicals (*The Greatest Showman*, *Wicked*)

Exercise/sports: Dance, spin class, CrossFit, exhibition sports and games with trophies, competitive lifting

Other Activities: Modeling, curating playlists or mood boards, self-care rituals, improv comedy, freestyle rap

Cocktail, Beer, and Wine Pairings for Boastful Assholes

Cocktail: Espresso Martini — chic, flashy, and makes a scene. Gives caffeine, glamour, and main character energy.

Beer: Hazy IPA — bold, juicy, and hyped to hell

Wine: Cabernet Sauvignon — flashy, expensive, unmistakable

Tips for Dealing with a Boastful Asshole

Working Relationships: Let them take credit when it doesn't cost you. Compliment publicly, correct privately. Link your goals to their visibility.

Domestic Relationships: Be an appreciative audience but also help them feel loved when they're not dazzling. Try to affirm their worth without inflating their ego.

Boastful Asshole Phrases

An easy way to identify a Boastful Asshole (other than having them take the quiz, which is the easiest) is when you hear them utter a phrase that reveals their intent. It is likely that someone saying one of these phrases has the Boastful trait in their profile as either their primary or secondary personality.

I'm not trying to brag, but... is a preamble to bragging, and they've probably rehearsed it a few times. Only the Peacock says this.

People are always asking me how I do it all. Wants everyone to acknowledge they are both high-achieving and mysteriously gifted.

I guess I have that energy people gravitate toward. It's time for a head nod or an amen here for validation. Multiple support emojis would also be acceptable.

Triggers for Boastful Assholes

The Peacock has emotional and situational triggers that can make them lose their composure, at least momentarily. The table below lists some common triggers and some ideas on how to calm their nerves during and after a triggering.

Trigger	Why it upsets them	How to ease their nerves
Being ignored	The Peacock needs visibility and validation on a primal level and ignoring can cause physical pain	Give them specific compliments that sound believable
Public criticism	They feel exponentially humiliated the more public the critique	Give critical feedback with respect, in private instead of airing grievances in front of others
Dismissing their achievements	Downplaying their accomplishments devalues their identity of success	Celebrate or at least acknowledge their achievements before moving on to other topics
Lack of an audience	Feeling invisible can trigger a gloom spiral	If they are lacking an audience today, create shareable wins they can take some credit for

Trigger	Why it upsets them	How to ease their nerves
A competing ego	Heavy competition by an individual who also has an audience can trigger insecurities	Remind them of their uniqueness

Love for Boastful Assholes

Best Match: Codependent Asshole

Why it works: Boastful craves admiration; Codependent lives to nurture and support. It's a validation loop of glamour and devotion. Codependent gets someone who needs love unconditionally; Boastful gets a personal fan club.

Bonus Love Spark: Instagram couple energy, endless selfies, matching outfits, over-posting.

Boastful Asshole Relationship Dynamics

The table below lists potential collaborations and pitfalls for the Boastful Asshole as they deal with each of the other assholes in the zodiac.

Assholes	Relationship Dynamic	Areas of Risk	Bonding Opportunities
Cynical Asshole (Cat)	The irony of glamour	Peacock feels judged	Peacocking together in a sarcastic way
Analytical Asshole (Falcon)	Flexing and fact-checks	Mutual irritation	Impressing others using logic, data, combined with a performative flair
Dramatic Asshole (Cockatoo)	Showbiz synergy	Competitive drama, collaborative meltdowns	Loud love and appreciation
Martyr Asshole (Elephant)	Sacrificing for the performance	Martyr feels invisible	Playing hero and victim together on a shared stage fuels both

Assholes	Relationship Dynamic	Areas of Risk	Bonding Opportunities
Stoic Asshole (Tortoise)	Beauty gets tedious	Stoic slowly withdraws out of boredom	Learning different types of grace from each other expands capabilities
Codependent Asshole (Golden Retriever)	Perfect worship dynamic	Codependent may lose themselves	Devotion and display of affection
Jester Asshole (Chimpanzee)	Loud, chaotic fun	May turn shallow	Public attention and private silliness
Bureaucratic Asshole (Beaver)	Rules tries to reign in the rebel	Peacock gets bored by rules	Bringing respectability through well-organized performances
Vanishing Asshole (Fox)	Catch me if you can	Ghosting triggers insecurity in Peacock	Romantic mystery games
Scheming Asshole (Octopus)	One dazzles as the other controls	Power struggle	Image crafting as a team
Sanctimonious Asshole (Owl)	Glitz and shame	Peacock feels condemned and defensive by shaming	Public service as social proof

Ideal Purpose and Life Journey for The Boastful Asshole

The ultimate life purpose for a Boastful Asshole is to inspire others to greatness by providing exposure and boosting their self-confidence. By sharing their spotlight with people who bring a positive impact (without eclipsing them with their brilliance) the Boastful Asshole gains the immortal influence they've been searching for all along.

Along the way they will gain momentum and insight by channeling their ambition to assist meaningful causes. They find that promoting others with sincerity helps transform their vanity into vision, while still providing the attention they crave.

Their successful journey begins as an ego-driven performer, oozing with confidence, but sensitive to ridicule. In the end, they deliver their masterful performance, not for the applause, but in order to elevate others with altruistic motives in way that satisfies their own ego instead of depleting it.

"Inside every cynical person is a disappointed idealist."

— George Carlin

The Cynical Asshole

Animal Spirit: Cat

Motivational Driver: Avoidance

Best Traits: Witty, unbothered

Worst Traits: Apathetic, unreliable

Cynical Asshole Profile

You're the cool philosopher, breezy, unbothered, and tuned into life's pleasures without being consumed by them. You possess a rare mix of wit and wisdom, often the first to see through illusions others cling to. You don't just live in the moment — you own it.

While some may think you're detached and hedonistic, it's only because you've learned to protect your peace. You're not lazy at all. You are discerning with your energy. Joy, aesthetics, and sharp insight are your trademarks. You turn existential dread into dark humor and small talk into intellectual rebellion. People are drawn to your vibe because you refuse to fake enthusiasm. Your authenticity is your aura. Whether lounging, or reading, or packing a knowing grin, you make it all look easy. You're the velvet glove on the hand that's flipping off the universe. Cool without trying, wise without preaching, and just distant enough to be missed. You're the storm in sunglasses.

Famous Cynical Assholes

The "Too-Cool-For-This" Philosopher: Witty, jaded, aloof

- Anthony Bourdain

- Oscar Wilde

- Fran Lebowitz

- Bill Maher

- George Carlin

Career Aptitude for Cynical Assholes

Cultural Critic / Satirist / Blogger: dissects hypocrisy with a smirk

UX Designer / Experience Consultant: sees through what people say and interprets what they want

Freelance Creative / Consultant: works best untethered

Art Director or Underground Filmmaker: feeds irony into aesthetics

Cynical Asshole Archetypes in Literature and Film

Rick Sanchez in *Rick and Morty*

Rick Blaine in *Casablanca*

Daria Morgendorffer in *Daria*

Tyler Durden in *Fight Club*

Best Entertainment for Cynical Assholes

Games: The Stanley Parable, Disco Elysium, Cards Against Humanity

Music: Lo-fi Hip Hop, Post-Punk, Grunge

Stories: Dry comedy, dark satire, existential indie films

Exercise/sports: Skateboarding, solo hiking, slacklining

Other Activities: Indulgent alone time with music or art, saying no and meaning no

Cocktail, Beer, and Wine Pairings for Cynical Assholes

Cocktail: Black Manhattan — Classic, brooding, and bitter in all the right ways; it says, "I'm drinking, but I'm not celebrating"

Beer: Dry Irish Stout — dark, dry, doesn't try too hard

Wine: Barolo — earthy, moody, and not here to please

Tips for Dealing with a Cynical Asshole

Working Relationships: Don't force positivity. Acknowledge their skepticism because that's how they guard themselves. Prove that you're competent and not easily rattled.

Domestic Relationships: Give them space, not pressure. Over-criticism will make them look for an exit. Cynicals bond through shared eye-rolls more than heart-to-heart discussions. Be steady, not needy.

Cynical Asshole Phrases

An easy way to identify a Cynical Asshole (other than having them take the quiz, which is the easiest) is when you hear them utter a phrase that reveals their intent. It is likely that someone saying one of these phrases has the Cynical trait in their profile as either their primary or secondary personality.

Must be nice to still believe. Reality ruined me but your hope is adorable.

I'm not being negative. I'm being realistic. Bitterness is the price for biting Eve's apple. They don't need you to hop off the optimist train, only to acknowledge that they have hopped already for good reasons that you may never grasp.

Good luck...seriously. They have no faith in what you are trying to accomplish, but pretending to be supportive is better than looking like an asshole, and they are not confident enough to burn this bridge.

Triggers for Cynical Assholes

The Cat has emotional and situational triggers that can make them lose their composure, at least momentarily. The table below lists some common triggers and some ideas on how to calm their nerves during and after a triggering.

Trigger	Why it upsets them	How to ease their nerves
Forced positivity	The stay positive philosophy feels fake and can grate on their nerves	Address the nuance of something positive instead of selling hope
Inspiring speeches	A long hurrah speech or monologue seems disingenuous, triggering an eye-rolling contempt	Use realism and practicality to present your case
Being told to 'lighten up'	"Lighten-up" feels condescending and dismissive — light is not what they do	Validate their perspective before shifting tone away from the obvious irony they've already pointed out
Blind optimism from others	Similar to forced positivity, blind optimism just feels naïve	Balance your message of hope with real evidence

Trigger	Why it upsets them	How to ease their nerves
Overeager social bonding	The Cat mistrusts your eagerness for their attention. It feels intrusive somehow	Let them warm up in their own time; If you have a ball of yarn they like (or hate), they'll play

Love for Cynical Assholes

Best Match: Jester Asshole

Why it works: Both the Cat and Chimpanzee run on wit, irreverence, and insight. Jester keeps Cynical laughing when the void gets too loud, and Cynical helps Jester feel seen beyond the punchlines. They're emotionally independent and intellectually intimate.

Bonus Love Spark: Sarcasm-fueled foreplay, dark jokes, intellectual sparing, deeply stoned debates.

Cynical Asshole Relationship Dynamics

The table below lists potential collaborations and pitfalls for the Cynical Asshole as they deal with each of the other assholes in the zodiac.

Assholes	Relationship Dynamic	Areas of Risk	Bonding Opportunities
Analytical Asshole (Falcon)	Cold, smart, detached	No emotional anchor either way	Debate-as-foreplay
Dramatic Asshole (Cockatoo)	Chaos and critique	Overwhelming situations, avoidance	Chemistry via passion/sarcasm combo
Martyr Asshole (Elephant)	Cynic retreats as Martyr clings	Guilt trip cycles	Shared existential suffering
Stoic Asshole (Tortoise)	Intellectual monks	Running out of sparks	Silence as intimacy

Assholes	Relationship Dynamic	Areas of Risk	Bonding Opportunities
Codependent Asshole (Golden Retriever)	Emotionally asymmetrical	Ghosting the giver	A feel good with slow-built trust and gentle landings
Jester Asshole (Chimpanzee)	Banter buddies	Staying surface-level without sharing vulnerability	Dark humor, chaotic flirting
Bureaucratic Asshole (Beaver)	Rules meets rebellion	Cynic mocks their beautiful system	System critiques
Vanishing Asshole (Fox)	Mutual detachment	Risk of emotional apathy	No-pressure connections
Scheming Asshole (Octopus)	Paranoia party	Mutual suspicion	Clever planning and unspoken truths
Sanctimonious Asshole (Owl)	Morality and mockery	Condescension wars	Philosophical debates
Boastful Asshole (Peacock)	Judgy vs. flashy	Mutual disdain	Secret attraction to confidence

Ideal Purpose and Life Journey for The Cynical Asshole

The ultimate life purpose for a Cynical Asshole is to alchemize their detachment into a radical presence that exposes serious hypocrisy and injustice with eloquence, guiding the masses toward revelation.

Along the way they will gain momentum and insight by reading and writing essays, scripts, reviewing art and short films that will help them develop their own voice, and by hosting debates and think-tanks in non-serious settings. Their transformation begins when they realize that mockery alone is hollow and learn that they have the skill and talent to build something, not just burn it down.

Their successful journey begins as an aloof rebel and emotionally armed observer that thrives on irony, sarcasm, and dark humor, but their viewpoint is often only viewed as disruptive or annoying. In the end, after honing their craft, they emerge as a wise illuminator with the skills to communicate their truth to a vast audience.

"In God we trust. All others must bring data."

— W. Edwards Deming

The Analytical Asshole

Animal Spirit: Falcon

Motivational Driver: Control

Best Traits: Honest, insightful

Worst Traits: Cutting, cold

Analytical Asshole Profile

You are the razor-sharp observer, analytical, insightful, and unwaveringly committed to truth. While others tiptoe around difficult topics, you stride through them, armed with logic and deadpan clarity. Your honesty is refreshing, even if it cuts deep. You simply don't see the point in sugarcoating because progress depends on truth. That's not cynical; you're just two steps ahead. People trust you because you say what others are too polite to admit.

Beneath your cool exterior lies a mind that's constantly refining ideas, seeking precision, and sharpening others by challenging them. While they may flinch at your critiques, they also secretly seek them out. You're the person who improves everything and everyone by being yourself.

You don't do drama; you do accuracy. You're not mean, you're correct. And that's your superpower. You are the scalpel that heals by cutting, that friend we need when we've all had enough lies.

Famous Analytical Assholes

The Cold Genius: Brutally honest, insightful, critical

- Stanley Kubrick

- Ayn Rand

- Jordan Peterson

- Noam Chomsky

- Marie Curie

Career Aptitude for Analytical Assholes

Data Scientist / Data Analyst: turns chaos into clear insight

Research Scientist / Detective thrives on truth and intellectual rigor

Architect: converting abstract problems into structured blueprints

Think Tank Consultant: blunt, brilliant, strategic

Analytical Asshole Archetypes in Literature and Film

Sherlock Holmes in the *Canon of Sherlock Holmes*

Dr. House in *House MD*

Lisbeth Salander in *The Girl with the Dragon Tattoo*

Lisa Simpson in *The Simpsons*

Best Entertainment for Analytical Assholes

Games: Logic puzzles

Music: Ambient Electronic, Minimalist Techno

Stories: Sci-Fi, complex literature, thought-driven documentaries

Exercise/sports: Solo walks or runs, rowing, weightlifting, golf

Other Activities: Deep focus time, cold showers

Cocktail, Beer, and Wine Pairings for Analytical Assholes

Cocktail: Dry Martini (extra cold, extra dry) — cold, complete, unforgiving. If you get it, you get it.

Beer: Pilsner — clean, precise, flawless execution

Wine: Riesling (dry) — laser-sharp, highly structured, brutally honest

Analytical Asshole Phrases

An easy way to identify an Analytical Asshole (other than having them take the quiz, which is the easiest) is when you hear them utter a phrase that reveals their intent. It is likely that someone saying one of these phrases has the Analytical trait in their profile as either their primary or secondary personality.

Let's focus on the facts. The Falcon is about to replace your argument with a dataset.

That's not technically correct. What you meant and what is said is different. It's their duty to correct the phraseology so that everyone is on the same page.

I don't make decisions based on feelings. They can quantify their own feelings in a chart if it really matters to you. But in general, feelings are a distraction to getting things done right to keep moving forward.

Triggers for Analytical Assholes

The Falcon has emotional and situational triggers that can make them lose their composure, at least momentarily. The table below lists some common triggers for Analytical personality types and some ideas on how to calm their nerves during and after a triggering.

Trigger	Why it upsets them	How to ease their nerves
Emotional appeals	An emotional appeal seems either irrational or manipulative or both	Translate an emotional reaction into a logical argument that they can follow
Last-minute changes	They spend a lot of time planning to requirements and last-minute changes disrupt their planning flow	Give them advanced notice and a logical structure for changes
Messy or vague communication	Ambiguity causes frustration	Use clear, concise language before the loose ends and chaos become overwhelming
Being micromanaged	Micromanaging undermines their known competence	Provide autonomy with a system of mutual accountability
Overly sentimental gestures	Extended sessions of gushy sentiment appears performative for no good reason	Keep praise and emotional displays sincere and straightforward

Love for Analytical Assholes

Best Match: Stoic Asshole

Why it works: Two minds, one quiet storm. Analytical dissects and Stoic endures. Together, they build trust through consistency and depth. This is the slow-burn duo that others mistake for emotionally unavailable — until they unleash power moves side by side.

Bonus Love Spark: Power silence, books in bed, no drama — just dominance.

Tips for Dealing with an Analytical Asshole

Working Relationships: Give them data, precision, and logic. Emotions are distractions unless they are charted in a spreadsheet. Be prepared to make your case before a meeting.

Domestic Relationships: Don't expect romance on demand. Earn intimacy through thoughtful discussions and structured problem-solving. They express love in spreadsheets and advice.

Analytical Asshole Relationship Dynamics

The table below lists potential collaborations and pitfalls for the Analytical Asshole as they deal with each of the other assholes in the zodiac.

Assholes	Relationship Dynamic	Areas of Risk	Bonding Opportunities
Dramatic Asshole (Cockatoo)	Feelings vs. facts	Emotional burnout	Complementary strengths in a crisis
Martyr Asshole (Elephant)	Planning to over-give	Passive-aggressive tension	Solving problems together
Stoic Asshole (Tortoise)	Mutual respect and restraint	Emotional avoidance, assumptions in silence	Peaceful co-existence
Codependent Asshole (Golden Retriever)	Analyst gets overwhelmed	Clinginess begs detachment	Teaching boundaries with clarity
Jester Asshole (Chimpanzee)	Chaos vs. logic	Chimp breaks all the rules for no apparent reason	Structured fun, mutual learning

Assholes	Relationship Dynamic	Areas of Risk	Bonding Opportunities
Bureaucratic Asshole (Beaver)	Rules meet systems	Overload of rigidity	Productive partnership
Vanishing Asshole (Fox)	Inconsistent connection	Ghosting disrupts planning time and schedules	Shared curiosity, quick small-talk free planning exercises, mystery-driven tension
Scheming Asshole (Octopus)	Calculated alliance	Power tension	Strategic collaboration
Sanctimonious Asshole (Owl)	Logic and ethics	Stubborn principals lead to unresolvable arguments	Debates on ethical data
Boastful Asshole (Peacock)	Flash meets function	Ego friction	Show-and-tell collaborations
Cynical Asshole (Cat)	Detached duo	Pessimism vortex	Intellectual sparring

Ideal Purpose and Life Journey for The Analytical Asshole

The ultimate life purpose for an Analytical Asshole is to evolve to market truth in service of love, instead of merely presenting data for the sake of logic or to win a debate.

Along the way they will gain momentum and insight by consulting or teaching in non-brutal environments, performing deep research or investigations, or complex design work intended to avoid impacts or that offers significant benefits to people they care about. They may also thrive at writing anonymous editorials, critiques, or whistleblowing blogs.

Their successful journey begins early as a cold-hearted truth teller, whose opinion is valued but sometimes too stressful to pursue for their wary peers. By working on their people-and communication skills, the Falcon learns to wield their intellect as a tool for transformation, to explain themselves without sounding judgy, and to progress healing without creating division.

"I feel there is something unexplored about woman that only a woman can explore."

— Georgia O'Keeffe

The Dramatic Asshole

Animal Spirit: Cockatoo

Motivational Driver: Performance

Best Traits: Empathic, expressive

Worst Traits: Manipulative, chaotic

Dramatic Asshole Profile

You feel deeply, live passionately, and connect intensely. Life for you is felt, not just lived. You have a remarkable ability to articulate emotional undercurrents and transform chaos into story. What some see as theatrical behavior is actually a superior tuning-in to the epic nature of existence.

Your openness to experience, especially painful experience, makes you incredibly relatable and magnetic. You don't just survive emotional storms. You turn them into poetry and song that electrifies the air. When you speak, others listen, because your vulnerability is your power, and your audience can't get enough. You make emotions fashionable. Your pain has style. People turn to you when they want raw, real, and unforgettable. Your ability to cast yourself as the protagonist is like an empathy locomotive. You bring color to grayscale worlds, tears to dull conversations, and meaning to messiness that would otherwise go unnoticed or dismissed as trivial. Your life is a feature film and the people around you are lucky to get a cameo appearance.

Famous Dramatic Assholes

The Emotional Hurricane: Expressive, chaotic, magnetic

- Britney Spears
- Marlon Brando
- Jim Morrison
- Roxxxy Andrews
- Amaya Espinal

Career Aptitude for Dramatic Assholes

Actor / Pop Star / Performance Artist: channels chaos into beauty

Teacher (English, Debate, or Creative Classes): brings flair to the classroom

Therapist: makes others feel deeply seen

Storyteller / Novelist: turns pain into narrative power

Dramatic Asshole Archetypes in Literature and Film

Moira Rose in *Schitt's Creek*

BoJack Horseman in *BoJack Horseman*

Elizabeth Wurtzel in *Prozac Nation*

Nina Sayers in *Black Swan*

Albert in *The Bird Cage*

Best Entertainment for Dramatic Assholes

Games: The Last of Us, Heavy Rain, Fiasco

Music: Art pop, theatrical and cinematic scores, 90s alternative angst

Stories: Emotional films and live theatre (A Star is Born, Les Misérables, Hamilton, Moulin Rouge)

Exercise/sports: Dance, yoga, pole work

Other Activities: Expressive journaling, poetry, singing in the car, crying in the bathtub

Cocktail, Beer, and Wine Pairings for Dramatic Assholes

Cocktail: Aperol Spritz (with edible glitter) — Loud, pretty, and emotionally unstable. It's both a statement and a meltdown.

Beer: Fruited Sour — colorful, loud, emotional rollercoaster

Wine: Rosé Champagne — sparkling, intense, theatrical

Tips for Dealing with a Dramatic Asshole

Working Relationships: Validate their emotional temperature. They need to be heard and seen. Show excitement for their ideas (but gently set limits).

Domestic Relationships: They crave attention but they also melt when given sincere emotional support. Laugh with them, listen to their chaos, and provide consistent affection.

Dramatic Asshole Phrases

An easy way to identify a Dramatic Asshole (other than having them take the quiz, which is the easiest) is when you hear them utter a phrase that reveals their intent. It is likely that someone saying one of these phrases has the Dramatic trait in their profile as either their primary or secondary personality.

I literally can't with this right now. Whatever is happening is too much to process without full emotional attention.

This always happens to me. Move in for the close-up on the tragic lead. Your support role is to gasp, comfort, and validate, in that order.

You don't get it. It's not just about that! They have layered seven emotional subplots to the topic at hand, and you do not appreciate all the nuances.

Triggers for Dramatic Assholes

The Cockatoo has emotional and situational triggers that can make them lose their composure, at least momentarily. The table below lists some common triggers and some ideas on how to calm their nerves during and after a triggering.

Trigger	Why it upsets them	How to ease their nerves
Emotional invalidation	They feel erased when their feelings are dismissed or minimalized	Acknowledge their feelings first before making any other point
Being interrupted	Their expressive flow is broken and capturing the mood of the message again is in jeopardy	Listen first before redirecting
Boredom from the audience	A yawn or fidget can look like rejection	Re-engage with a passionate topic
Conflict avoidance	The Cockatoo needs an emotional release. If you walk away you're causing them physical pain	Allow their expression but set limits
Being told to calm down	The words "calm down" is punch of dismissiveness after a triggering	Use grounding language and techniques instead like doing breathing exercises together

Love for Dramatic Assholes

Best Match: Boastful Asshole

Why it works: Both live for performance, emotion, and being seen. Boastful brings glamor; Dramatic brings depth. They'll fight like hell and love like fireworks. If they don't implode this pair becomes legend.

Bonus Love Spark: Shared public meltdowns, grand romantic gestures, shared Spotify playlists of heartbreak songs.

Dramatic Asshole Relationship Dynamics

The table below lists potential collaborations and pitfalls for the Dramatic Asshole as they deal with each of the other assholes in the zodiac.

Assholes	Relationship Dynamic	Areas of Risk	Bonding Opportunities
Martyr Asshole (Elephant)	Feeds on emotional intensity	One collapses as the other explodes in a cycle of peaks and valleys	Deep emotional validation
Stoic Asshole (Tortoise)	Still water meets hurricane	Emotional disconnection	Learning balance through a sincere character study of opposites
Codependent Asshole (Golden Retriever)	Emotional overdrive	Both lack boundaries	Intense loyalty and caretaking
Jester Asshole (Chimpanzee)	Theater kids in love	Chaos becomes amplified and there's no control switch	Shared love of spotlight and attention
Bureaucratic Asshole (Beaver)	Drama meets policy	Constant resistance	Collaborate in creative constraint and comic tension

Assholes	Relationship Dynamic	Areas of Risk	Bonding Opportunities
Vanishing Asshole (Fox)	Abandonment triggers	Fox disappears mid-Cockatoo meltdown	Chemistry through contrast and troubadour scenarios
Scheming Asshole (Octopus)	Emotional chaos dives into the cold plan	Mismatched expression	Manipulation strategy to include emotion
Sanctimonious Asshole (Owl)	Moral rigidity accented by drama	Cockatoo hates a judgmental tone and Owl can't help it	Righteous performance alliances
Boastful Asshole (Peacock)	Competitively loud	Ego wars	Dynamic duets
Cynical Asshole (Cat)	Open heart meets closed system	Shared emotional shutdowns	Drama and creative detachment begets storytelling sparks
Analytical Asshole (Falcon)	Feelings vs. facts	Dramatic feels unseen	Complementary crisis response

Ideal Purpose and Life Journey for The Dramatic Asshole

The ultimate life purpose for a Dramatic Asshole is to humanize suffering through storytelling, art, and presence, turning vulnerability into collective healing in a way that resonates with non-dramatic assholes.

Along the way they will gain momentum and insight by participating in performing arts, emotional coaching, and documenting the human condition. They will feel more pain than any other personality type, but they can learn to use the pain, to recycle it, and make it meaningful for themselves and for others. They are the first to cry so that others will know it's okay to cry at all.

Their successful journey begins with emotional chaos and judgment by others who fail to understand why they can't get their feelings under control, labeling them "too much" or "needy." It progresses to a skillful performance of conscious empathy, featuring emotion as a divine language, more sincere and impactful than any other form of communication. Their story arc ends when they can clearly see that they were never "too much;" they were exactly what was needed when the world forgot how to feel.

"I have given everything. There is nothing left."

— King Lear, Shakespeare

The Martyr Asshole

Animal Spirit: Elephant

Motivational Driver: Control

Best Traits: Loyal, hardworking

Worst Traits: Resentful, controlling

Martyr Asshole Profile

You are the unsung hero, the one who gives selflessly, supports, and endures as others fold and fall away. Reliable to a fault, you're the glue holding everyone together. You don't just show up...you stay.

While some people think you are intense or overbearing, you simply care too much to let things fall apart. Your sacrifices are legendary, and your loyalty is fierce. You take on more than your share not for praise, glory, or profit, but because you can. When others need help, you're there, often before they even ask. People may not always appreciate your devotion, but they always need it. You are a fortress in human form, and your quiet strength shapes worlds. You are not a doormat. People need to see that. You are the foundation upon which successful systems are built and the constant that enables their operation.

Your inner fire burns hottest when you're protecting those you love, even if they don't know they're being shielded. In the story of others' success, you're the unnamed engine that makes it all possible.

Famous Martyr Assholes

The Burnt-Out Hero: Over-giving, resentful

- Mother Teresa
- John McCain
- Joan of Arc
- Meghan Markle
- Huda Mustafa

Career Aptitude for Martyr Assholes

Project Manager: holds it all together behind the scenes

Nurse / Caretaker / Emergency Responder: always shows up, no matter the toll

Social Worker / Therapist / Crisis Coordinator: takes on heavy emotional lifting

Community Organizer: quietly brings society together

Martyr Asshole Archetypes in Literature and Film

Katniss Everdeen in *The Hunger Games*

Severus Snape in *Harry Potter*

Samwise Gamgee in *The Lord of the Rings*

Annie in *Hereditary*

Best Entertainment for Martyr Assholes

Games: The Sims and other world building games that require maintenance, Mass Effect Trilogy, Keep Talking and Nobody Explodes

Music: Folk Rock, Heartland Americana

Stories: Family sagas, romances, blue-collar tragedies

Exercise/sports: Team sports, bootcamp, high-effort cardio, 5Ks for charity

Other Activities: Charity events and volunteering, exploring emotional meaning at museums and galleries, quality time with pets and animal rescues, self-help books, spa day

Cocktail, Beer, and Wine Pairings for Martyr Assholes

Cocktail: Hot Toddy— Warm, healing, and a little old-school. The cocktail that shows up when you're sick, tired, or heartbroken, even if no one asks for it.

Beer: Brown Ale — dependable, toasty, overlooked

Wine: Merlot — soft, hardworking, too often dismissed

Tips for Dealing with a Martyr Asshole

Working Relationships: Acknowledge their stellar self-motivation and effort, even if it's overdone. Help them set boundaries in advance without shaming them for over-functioning.

Domestic Relationships: They need to feel needed — but not exploited. Give appreciation, ask how you can help (for once), and stop treating their love like a utility.

Martyr Asshole Phrases

An easy way to identify a Martyr Asshole (other than having them take the quiz, which is the easiest) is when you hear them utter a phrase that reveals their intent. It is likely that someone saying one of these phrases has the Martyr trait in their profile as either their primary or secondary personality.

Of course I volunteered. No one else was going to step up. Elephants are prone to obligation. Their simple reward is feeling morally superior to you and anyone who didn't volunteer. Don't mess that up for them.

It's fine. I'll handle it...like I always do. They are exhausted from doing everything for everyone and looking for you to express some guilt ASAP.

They don't realize how much I do for them. Their identity is framed on being needed, but they'll spiral into resentment when they are not shown proper appreciation.

Triggers for Martyr Assholes

The Elephant has emotional and situational triggers that can make them lose their composure, at least momentarily. The table below lists some common triggers and some ideas on how to calm their nerves during and after a triggering.

Trigger	Why it upsets them	How to ease their nerves
Unappreciated effort	The Elephant's self-worth revolves around being needed and appreciation is their fuel and reward	Thank them sincerely and often
Being told to 'let it go'	"Let it go" feels like their pain is being dismissed as unimportant	Acknowledge their effort and sacrifice before trying to redirect
Others not helping enough	Being the lone volunteer for a task triggers over-functioning, and soon after, resentment	Watch their moves and offer support before they break
Being misunderstood	Not comprehending *why* they are upset undermines their sacrifice narrative, as if you didn't even notice their effort	"I'm sorry" is not enough; Repeat back their concerns in earnest with empathy

Trigger	Why it upsets them	How to ease their nerves
Accusations of manipulation	Accusing them of being manipulative hits a moral blind spot that can shut them down	Frame your feedback as concern, not as blame

Love for Martyr Assholes

Best Match: Sanctimonious Asshole

Why it works: Both Martyr and Sanctimonious need purpose and appreciation. They see each other's pain and principles as sacred.

Bonus Love Spark: Sunday mornings full of lists, service projects, and shared indignation.

Martyr Asshole Relationship Dynamics

The table below lists potential collaborations and pitfalls for the Martyr Asshole as they deal with each of the other assholes in the zodiac.

Assholes	Relationship Dynamic	Areas of Risk	Bonding Opportunities
Stoic Asshole (Tortoise)	Martyr nurtures while Stoic endures	The Elephant gives too much and the Tortoise gives too little	Deep loyalty over time
Codependent Asshole (Golden Retriever)	Guilt meets need	Mutual burnout risk	Shared care-taking mission
Jester Asshole (Chimpanzee)	Self-sacrifice vs. self-expression	Martyr feels unseen	Joyful emotional healing
Bureaucratic Asshole (Beaver)	Service meets structure	Martyr resents inflexible systems	Steady teamwork, especially under pressure

Assholes	Relationship Dynamic	Areas of Risk	Bonding Opportunities
Vanishing Asshole (Fox)	Abandonment nightmare	Fox's emotional withdrawal hurts Martyr deeply	Forgiveness and silent understanding
Scheming Asshole (Octopus)	Martyr gets played	Imbalance of power	Collaborating on shared sacrifice goals
Sanctimonious Asshole (Owl)	Elephant seeks a purpose and Owl provides it	Co-enabling extremes	Righteous partnership
Boastful Asshole (Peacock)	Martyr feels used	Recognition disparity	Acts of service meet public validation
Cynical Asshole (Cat)	Martyr gives while Cynic mocks	Emotional injury	Bonding over shared pain
Analytical Asshole (Falcon)	Heart meets head	Miscommunication	Organizing healing experiences together
Dramatic Asshole (Cockatoo)	Martyr absorbs everything	Emotional overflow	Codependent performance duo

Ideal Purpose and Life Journey for The Martyr Asshole

The ultimate life purpose for a Martyr Asshole is to uplift others (without abandoning themselves) and build a legacy through service-based leadership.

Along the way they will gain momentum and insight by creating boundaries for themselves while supporting others through teaching, advising, or caregiving, learning to say "no" without guilt, and naming their hidden resentments sooner than later to prevent stewing grudges and avoid making the more aloof personalities want to run from perceived emotional blackmail. Eventually they will learn that boundaries are an act of love, for themselves and others.

Their successful journey begins with self-sacrifice and over-volunteering, often underappreciated by the beneficiaries of their work. In the end they are instrumental in creating enduring service systems that help people and causes, without sacrificing themselves or others. They are able to recognize proper boundaries before planning tasks, and able to serve from the fulness of their heart without stress and depletion.

"Silence is a source of great strength."

— Lao Tzu

The Stoic Asshole

Animal Spirit: Tortoise

Motivational Driver: Control

Best Traits: Calm, strategic

Worst Traits: Dismissive, stonewalling

Stoic Asshole Profile

Calm, composed, and impossible to rattle, you are the master of silent strength. You don't waste words or energy, and you prefer to let your quiet presence speak for itself. You outlast the drama, knowing that when the tide rolls out again, you'll still be here, the same steadfast pillar that has always held up the peer.

Some people find you aloof or hard to read. That's because you don't feel the need to be constantly understood. You are the eye of the storm, grounded and unshakable. You have a monkish patience with unmatched emotional discipline. When others are reactive, you retreat, assess, and return to the subject on your own terms with a superior perspective. People mislabel your detachment as coldness, but really, this is your form of respect for yourself and others…why respond emotionally on impulse before measuring the issue and calculating the right response? It is in that stillness where your power lies. You never explode — you endure. In a loud world, you remain above the noise and embody the final word, even when you don't speak.

Famous Stoic Assholes

The Stone Wall: Detached, calm, unreadable

- Clint Eastwood

- Greta Garbo

- Marcus Aurelius

- Queen Elizabeth II

- Keanu Reeves

Career Aptitude for Stoic Assholes

Engineer / Architect builds with logic and poise.

Judge / Negotiator / Mediator: calm in emotional storms, doesn't flinch.

Military Officer / Security Analyst: unflinching under pressure.

Stoic Asshole Architypes in Literature and Film

Mr. Spock in *Star Trek*

Lady Jessica in *Dune*

Clarisse Starling in *The Silence of the Lambs*

Michael Corleone in *The Godfather Part II*

Raymond Holt in *Brooklyn Nine-Nine*

Best Entertainment for Stoic Assholes

Games: Strategy games, crossword puzzles, Sudoku

Music: Post-Rock and Instrumental Metal (like Apocalyptica)

Stories: Samurai stories, historical fiction and non-fiction, documentaries, Neo-Noir films (like Blade Runner and Heat)

Exercise/sports: Hiking, Tai Chi, long-distance cycling, rowing crew, yoga

Other Activities: Solo drives, silent retreats, rare collections, gardening, woodworking, meditation

Cocktail, Beer, and Wine Pairings for Stoic Assholes

Cocktail: Single Malt Whiskey (neat, with a drop of distilled water) — Minimalist. Strong. Zero show. Doesn't care if you're impressed — and that's what makes it hot.

Beer: Smoked Porter — deep, quiet, full of character

Wine: Syrah — dark, structured, unshakable

Tips for Dealing with a Stoic Asshole

Working Relationships: Give them time and space. Don't push for fast decisions or emotional reactions. Respect their rhythm and follow through on promises.

Domestic Relationships: Consistency over intensity. Show up. Don't dig for vulnerability — they'll offer it voluntarily if they don't feel pressured to confess.

Stoic Asshole Phrases

An easy way to identify a Stoic Asshole (other than having them take the quiz, which is the easiest) is when you hear them utter a phrase that reveals their intent. It is likely that someone saying one of these phrases has the Stoic trait in their profile as either their primary or secondary personality.

It's not that deep. Stoics want to focus on the simplest answer for their own sanity. They are uncomfortable with emotional intensity and want to demote problems from a big deal down to a small thing to halt the anxiety.

You don't need to prove anything to me. Your whole performance is landing on deaf ears. The Tortoise is uninterested in your emotional reasoning and wants you to do what you think you need to do without disturbing their ether any further.

I don't see the point in talking about it again. Closure seems less efficient than just pretending it never happened and moving forward.

Triggers for Stoic Assholes

The Tortoise has emotional and situational triggers that can make them lose their composure, at least momentarily. The table below lists some common triggers and some ideas on how to calm their nerves during and after a triggering.

Trigger	Why it upsets them	How to ease their nerves
Forced emotional sharing	Coaxing a Tortoise to express their emotions seems invasive to them and would be disingenuously performative	Let them open up on their own timeline or ask them their opinion without using the "feel" word
Chaotic environments	They may get overwhelmed in a rambunctious crowd as it disrupts their sense of control and calm	Provide structure and predictability when entering a chaotic environment
Being rushed	Unexpected rushing or adding to the scope last-minute interferes with their planned process	Create deadlines with some breathing room
Disregard for their routine	Feels disrespectful and upsets their protocol, introducing a fear that other things may go awry too	If a change is needed, allow them time to replan and adjust to new variables
Emotional outbursts	Shouting, crying, or other unexpected outbursts can shut them down emotionally or inspire retreat	Try to address them calmly and at low volume

Love for Stoic Assholes

Best Love Match: Bureaucratic Asshole

Why it works: Both Bureaucratic and Stoic appreciate dependability, planning, and emotional consistency. Their partnership is forged with mutual respect and a shared obsession with order. It's a systematic love where everyone knows the rules and no one is really surprised, (even if they say they are for conversational effect).

Bonus Love Sparks: They fall in love watching each other do things correctly without drama: fixing the entire mess without saying a word, sorting the chaos, preparing a complex cocktail, summarizing, alphabetizing, etc.

Stoic Asshole Relationship Dynamics

The table below lists potential collaborations and pitfalls for the Stoic Asshole as they deal with each of the other assholes in the zodiac.

Assholes	Relationship Dynamic	Areas of Risk	Bonding Opportunities
Codependent Asshole (Golden Retriever)	A calm cling	Each gets overwhelmed (at different times)	Quiet reassurance and gentle loyalty
Jester Asshole (Chimpanzee)	Stillness attends sparkle	Misreading each other	Slow and steady trust building and unexpected laughter
Bureaucratic Asshole (Beaver)	Stable duo	Risk of rut or non-productivity	Dependable rhythms and shared structures to make life easier
Vanishing Asshole (Fox)	Withdrawal match	Ghosting wars	Unspoken understanding
Scheming Asshole (Octopus)	Subtle vs. overt strategies	Passive-aggressive tension	Long-game power couple
Sanctimonious Asshole (Owl)	Mutual restraint	Owl's rigid moralism can burden or escalate if it goes on too long	Discipline and duty alignment

Assholes	Relationship Dynamic	Areas of Risk	Bonding Opportunities
Boastful Asshole (Peacock)	Style with substance	Tortoise tunes out and Peacock feels ignored	Teaching patience and teaching presence at the same time
Cynical Asshole (Cat)	Quiet pessimism	Emotional flatline	Intellectual minimalism
Analytical Asshole (Falcon)	Still logic	Emotional stasis	Peaceful and orderly coexistence
Dramatic Asshole (Cockatoo)	Opposites collide	Stoic overstimulation	Grounding and channeling emotional energy
Martyr Asshole (Elephant)	Nurture beckons retreat	Stoic appears ungrateful	Devotion and quiet support

Ideal Purpose and Life Journey for The Stoic Asshole

The ultimate life purpose for a Stoic Asshole is to use their natural ability to separate their actions from external and internal stimuli to lead people calmly during a significant crisis and/or share their gifts of emotional resilience with people engulfed in chaos.

Along the way they will gain momentum and insight by using their powers of perception to meditate, exploring the depth of their own emotions, and practice stillness with purpose. They learn to melt the severity of their instinctive detachment that makes them useful in high-stress situations but tedious in intimate ones. They train in types of crisis management, writing, and teaching to acquire the empathy and communication skills to let down their guard and interact with people who are more tightly tethered to their emotions.

Their successful journey begins with a cold, emotionally contained, and seemingly arrogant demeanor that keeps many people at arm's length. By exploring their own emotional repression and vulnerabilities they learn to understand how emotions affect thoughts and behaviors, both the good and the bad. By the end of their journey, they attain a wise stewardship that seems more inviting than judgmental, and they offer strategies for summoning the still strength that can provide much needed peace in a reactive world.

"I'm not upset that you lied to me. I'm upset that from now on, I can't believe you."

— Friedrich Nietzsche

The Codependent Asshole

Spirit Animal: Golden Retriever

Motivational Driver: Avoidance

Best Traits: Loyal, nurturing

Worst Traits: Smothering, needy

Codependent Asshole Profile

You are warm, nurturing, fiercely devoted and emotional glue in any group. You care deeply and love hard, often putting others' needs before your own with open-hearted generosity. Your strength lies in your willingness to stay when things get difficult and you have a natural instinct to nurture even while others withdraw. Less empathetic types may accuse you of being clingy, but you know instinctively when you're needed even if no one else does.

You are always in tune with those you love, often before they are. When they detach, you dive deeper. Your gift is emotional availability combined with sincere commitment, and it's the reason people feel safe around you. You thrive in connection with the people around you and always give more than you take (of course, you'll make sure to remind them). Your relationship bonds are lifelines for the people you chose to grace with your attention. You bring comfort, loyalty, and intimacy in a way most people can only dream of. You are love, turned up to 11.

Famous Codependent Assholes

The Over-Lover: Nurturing, needs to be needed

- Florence Nightingale

- Pete Davidson

- Will Smith

- Adele

- Kourtney Kardashian

Career Aptitude for Codependent Assholes

Teacher (especially early education): devoted to development

Nurse / Healer / Caregiver: endless emotional bandwidth

Social Work / Therapy: equipped to help people when they need it

Customer Success Manager: interprets needs before they're spoken

Codependent Asshole Archetypes in Literature and Film

Bella Swan in *Twilight*

Ted Mosby in *How I Met Your Mother*

Ross Geller in *Friends*

Frodo Baggins in *The Lord of the Rings*

Bridget Jones in *Bridget Jones's Diary*

Best Entertainment for Codependent Assholes

Games: Collaborative games (Dungeons and Dragons, Pandemic, The Voting Game)

Music: Soul, R&B ballads, soft rock, love songs

Stories: Romance and romantic comedies with emotional depth

Exercise/sports: Partner workouts (sweating together), group classes, dog walking

Other Activities: Hosting dinner parties, long therapeutic phone calls, baking/cooking, crafts, attending support circles, spa days, journaling feelings that aren't theirs, saying "I love you" to people, animals, and plants

Cocktail, Beer, and Wine Pairings for Codependent Assholes

Cocktail: Spiked Chai Latte — sweet, cozy, and nurturing. It tastes like "I made this for us"

Beer: Cream Ale — smooth, comforting, easy to love

Wine: Pinot Grigio — friendly, nurturing, a little clingy when warm

Tips for Dealing with a Codependent Asshole

Working Relationships: Be kind but clear. It's their nature to take on too much to try to please you. Encourage them to advocate for themselves. They confuse criticism with rejection, so be gentle or lighthearted in your delivery.

Domestic Relationships: Set boundaries up front. Try to be consistent voicing your desires and feelings, because they are paying close attention. Reassure them that they're loved and appreciated.

Codependent Asshole Phrases

An easy way to identify a Codependent Asshole (other than having them take the quiz, which is the easiest) is when you hear them utter a phrase that reveals their intent. It is likely that someone saying one of these phrases has the Codependent trait in their profile as either their primary or secondary personality.

I just want you to be happy. The Golden Retriever has completely abandoned their own needs to support you, hoping you'll them love them more for it.

I didn't want to bother you… They are afraid that you're going to pull away as soon as they ask you something (while you're enjoying time away from them for some reason).

I feel like I care so much more than other people. Their over-functioning is getting to them and there's a bitterness creeping in after realizing their gestures of affection have not been reciprocated.

Triggers for Codependent Assholes

The Golden Retriever has emotional and situational triggers that can make them lose their composure, at least momentarily. The table below lists some common triggers and some ideas on how to calm their nerves during and after a triggering.

Trigger	Why it upsets them	How to ease their nerves
Rejection or disapproval	Shakes their identity as "the good one"	Reaffirm their value before starting to critique
Being left out	Retrievers can have abandonment anxiety	Proactively invite them, include them, and check-in
Not being needed	Not having a purpose makes them feel restless or melancholy	Ask for help (even if it's symbolic) and you may get added value you didn't count on
Accusations of clinginess	The "clingy" word shames their connection style and they can over withdraw from worry	Talk about boundaries instead and reassure them that they are appreciated

Trigger	Why it upsets them	How to ease their nerves
Sudden emotional withdrawal	The cold-shoulder treatment feels like punishment	Clarify that you need some space without detaching emotionally

Love for Codependent Assholes

Best Love Match: Martyr Asshole

Why it works: Codependent and Martyr share emotional labor and are capable of growing healthy boundaries together. Both care "too much" and experience affection through emotional exhaustion. Together they can create a psychic balance that will endure.

Bonus Love Sparks: Both insist the other deserves more attention, comfort, foot rubs, forgiveness, etc. It becomes a competitive affection spiral that keeps them both feeling cherished and indispensable.

Codependent Asshole Relationship Dynamics

The table below lists potential collaborations and pitfalls for the Codependent Asshole as they deal with each of the other assholes in the zodiac.

Assholes	Relationship Dynamic	Areas of Risk	Bonding Opportunities
Jester Asshole (Chimpanzee)	Follower of the free spirit	Emotional rollercoaster	Laughing through insecurities
Bureaucratic Asshole (Beaver)	Supportive meets structured	Codependent feels choked	Loyalty through routine
Vanishing Asshole (Fox)	Chasing the escape artist	Emotional abandonment	Fleeting moments of peace in independence
Scheming Asshole (Octopus)	Giver meets strategist	Emotional manipulation finally comes to light	Devotion to direction

Assholes	Relationship Dynamic	Areas of Risk	Bonding Opportunities
Sanctimonious Asshole (Owl)	Seeks approval, receives judgment	Retriever gets self-esteem hit	Shared service orientation
Boastful Asshole (Peacock)	Worship and appreciation	Mindless exploitation	Confidence boost through genuine praise
Cynical Asshole (Cat)	Emotional misalignment	Retriever overextends with no reward	Slow trust-building and acceptance
Analytical Asshole (Falcon)	Logic vs. emotion	Retriever feels dismissed	Both learning self-regulation and discipline
Dramatic Asshole (Cockatoo)	Chaos magnets	Overwhelming intensity	Raw emotional bonding
Martyr Asshole (Elephant)	Rescue fantasy	Mutual burnout	Purpose-driven partnership
Stoic Asshole (Tortoise)	Gentle but distant	Fear of neglect, loneliness in proximity	Quiet, appreciative devotion over time

Ideal Purpose and Life Journey for The Codependent Asshole

The ultimate life purpose for a Codependent Asshole is to nurture relationships rooted in authenticity and mutual empowerment that produces soulful love (without possession).

Along the way they will gain momentum and insight by learning emotional boundaries, spending time alone intentionally and fruitfully, and applying their compassion to occupations for which appreciation is seldom available as fuel. With a deep understanding of "self" and a wise observance of the boundaries of others, their caregiving talents become the destination that satisfies as opposed to a bullseye to love and admiration.

Their successful journey begins by clinging to one or more connections, dismissive of toxic behaviors, attempting to weaponize their sadness for attention, or rationalizing unrequited loves. In the end, they cultivate inclusive communities and discover they have the power to create soulful relationships that do not oscillate with their measure of self-worth. They evolve as angels who dwell above the realms of guilt or insecurity, able to identify the people who can fulfill their immediate needs and help build mutually beneficial bonds, absent the assumptions or conditions that lead to disappointment. They are able to say "no" without guilt, and they are able to teach others like themselves to do the same.

"If you're going to tell people the truth, be funny or they'll kill you."

— Billy Wilder

The Jester Asshole

Animal Spirit: Chimpanzee

Motivational Driver: Performance

Best Traits: Clever, entertaining

Worst Traits: Cruel, deflecting

Jester Asshole Profile

Behold the life of the party! The clever spark! The one who always knows exactly what to say…even when you shouldn't. You are comedy with consequences.

Your humor is your sword and shield, slicing through tension with a grin, and raising spirits while keeping everyone on their toes. You are brilliantly observant and quick, using wit to challenge hypocrisy, expose pretension, or merely break the monotony. People have accused you of being mean, but your aim is to illuminate or lighten, not to hurt. Your gift is for turning truth into laughter and laughter into truth. You keep things moving. If the world is a circus, you are the ringmaster with a smile and a dagger.

Mischievous, sure. But malicious? Only when it's deserved. You're not here to play nice. You're here to play smart. People laugh because you are funny. They remember you because you're dangerous.

Famous Jester Assholes

The Knife-Wit: Funny, biting, deflective

- Joan Rivers
- Ricky Gervais
- Tina Fey
- Robin Williams
- Miley Cyrus

Career Aptitude for Jester Assholes

Comedian / Satirist: truth disguised as laughter

Advertising Copywriter: punches hard with few words

Talk Show Host / YouTuber / Podcaster: entertains and critiques at once

Jester Asshole Archetypes in Literature and Film

Deadpool in *Deadpool*

Wednesday Addams in *The Addams Family*

Ferris Bueller in *Ferris Bueller's Day Off*

Tyrion Lannister in *Game of Thrones*

Best Entertainment for Jester Assholes

Games: Jackbox Party Packs, Among Us, Coup, Overcooked

Music: Ska, humorous rap (Pete & Bas), parody pop (Weird Al Yankovich, Nice Peter)

Stories: Satire, black comedies, absurdist farce (Monty Python)

Exercise/sports: Parkour, dance battles, dodgeball, exhibition games (Globetrotters)

Other Activities: comedy posts and memes, podcasts, roasting friends who can take it, dance breaks

Cocktail, Beer, and Wine Pairings for Jester Assholes

Cocktail: Jungle Bird — Fruity, colorful, and deceivingly strong. She looks silly and hits hard.

Beer: Mexican Lager with lime — zippy, funny, deceptively sharp

Wine: Lambrusco — fizzy, red, weird, joyful chaos

Tips for Dealing with a Jester Asshole

Working Relationships: Keep things light but focused. Humor is their shield and they respect those who can play along but still get results. Give them boundaries without being emotional about it, lest you become a target of their truth telling.

Domestic Relationships: Laugh with them, not at them. They will open up emotionally, but it will be disguised as a quip. Don't punish their joy.

Jester Asshole Phrases

An easy way to identify a Jester Asshole (other than having them take the quiz, which is the easiest) is when you hear them utter a phrase that reveals their intent. It is likely that someone saying one of these phrases has the Jester trait in their profile as either their primary or secondary personality.

Relax, I'm joking. The insult was real, but the delivery was inspired by sitcom banter and they didn't mean for you to take it heart. Call them out and they'll pretend you're the uptight one for having no sense of humor.

I'm not dramatic — I just have good timing. The Chimp creates scenes based on current conversations happening around them as if we're all participating in a reality improv show. You've been playing your part beautifully, by the way.

My coping mechanism is humor…and wine. Mostly wine. They are lightly signaling that stress has a major impact on them, but making you laugh is better therapy in the moment than talking about it seriously, which is a major downer.

Triggers for Jester Assholes

The Chimpanzee has emotional and situational triggers that can make them lose their composure, at least momentarily. The table below lists some common triggers and some ideas on how to calm their nerves during and after a triggering.

Trigger	Why it upsets them	How to ease their nerves
Being taken too seriously	Misinterpreting a joke for a serious comment threatens their identity	Play along and pivot as needed
Long solemnity	The weight of a long somber vibe is suffocating	When unavoidable, add playful breaks
Harsh criticism	Personal criticism can wound beneath the shield of humor, initiating escape	Give soft corrections instead
Being ignored	The Jester needs a feedback loop to maintain their energy	Invite light input even when you don't want it from them
Abrupt seriousness	Suddenly moving to a dead serious agenda after a lighthearted discord feels like a rejection	More playful breaks

Love for Jester Assholes

Best Match: Boastful Asshole

Why it works: Jester and Boastful both feed off attention with a flair for the spotlight and a duty to performance. Neither takes emotional intensity very seriously. They learn to turn their charm and wit on together in a sort of balanced dance musical that appears scripted.

Bonus Love Sparks: Surprise role plays with improv-worthy skits. Cracking each other up with inside jokes. In public they flirt using competitive banter that makes onlookers feel both nervous and aroused.

Jester Asshole Relationship Dynamics

The table below lists potential collaborations and pitfalls for the Jester Asshole as they deal with each of the other assholes in the zodiac.

Assholes	Relationship Dynamic	Areas of Risk	Bonding Opportunities
Bureaucratic Asshole (Beaver)	Rules rebellion	Jester resists structure	Humor lightens the load
Vanishing Asshole (Fox)	Flirtation and frustration	Jester chases mystery	Teasing each other
Scheming Asshole (Octopus)	Chaos distracts strategy	Octopus suspects Chimp is unreliable and may be wary of their unpredictability	Jester provides strategic cover for Schemer's subtle moves
Sanctimonious Asshole (Owl)	Trickster meets preacher	Owl over-moralizes Chimpanzee's impulsive antics	Ethics through comedy
Boastful Asshole (Peacock)	Showbiz siblings	Competitive egos	Entertaining the world together with laughter and style

Assholes	Relationship Dynamic	Areas of Risk	Bonding Opportunities
Cynical Asshole (Cat)	Wit and sarcasm	Escalating nihilism can create emotional gaps or lead to depression	Side-by-side roasts
Analytical Asshole (Falcon)	Data subjected to impulse	Logic can kill the joy	Teaching each other flexibility with perspective
Dramatic Asshole (Cockatoo)	Theater overload	Emotional overdrive	Pure performance chemistry
Martyr Asshole (Elephant)	Levity vs. heaviness	Jester avoids guilt	Finding emotional balance and stress relief through laughter
Stoic Asshole (Tortoise)	Stillness meets chaos	Jester feels unseen	Earned warmth and quiet companionship between attempted jokes
Codependent Asshole (Golden Retriever)	Performer and cheerleader	Emotional imbalances	Shared laughter and loyalty

Ideal Purpose and Life Journey for The Jester Asshole

The ultimate life purpose for a Jester Asshole is to provide truth disguised as entertainment in a way that changes the perception of the masses. They hone their craft to serve a higher purpose, providing razor-sharp observations and jovial wisdom that causes people to laugh and think at the same time.

Along the way they will gain momentum and insight practicing their delivery and subject matter with diverse audiences to gauge reactions, measure their impact, and revise their message. They face their own insecurities by purging them with the same wit they use to disrupt the discourse around them. Eventually they discover a topic that they take seriously enough to study, leaving no stone unturned in exploring its associated injustices and peculiarities, all the while keeping their delivery light and playful.

Their successful journey begins as a class clown, feeding off the energy their disruption provides, and using humor as an armor against vulnerability. In the end, they become a divine disruptor, using humor and irony as holy fire to burn away hypocrisy and invite an awakening through laughter and discomfort. The refined delivery is what makes them immortal.

"Order is heaven's first law."

— Alexander Pope

The Bureaucratic Asshole

Animal Spirit: Beaver

Motivational Driver: Moral Enforcement

Best Traits: Responsible, structured

Worst Traits: Rigid, power-tripping

Bureaucratic Asshole Profile

You are the stability in a chaotic world: reliable, principled, and endlessly organized. You believe in the wisdom of structure, the virtue of order, and the dignity of tradition. As the backbone of any organization, you're the authority that keeps the world moving properly. You never bend to chaos — you correct it.

Rules are not cages to you. The rules are safety nets, a scaffolding for greatness. You don't just follow them, you plan them, enforce them, embody them, and improve them.

You ooze consistency, foresight, and expertise. You are dependable to the letter, loyal by contract, and precise in all things. People who call you rigid lack your clarity of purpose. Others seek your approval because it feels to them like passing a test. They may not all like you, but they will always need you. You are the quiet force keeping the universe from unraveling.

Famous Bureaucratic Assholes

The Rules Lawyer: Orderly, rigid, authority-bound

- J. Edgar Hoover

- Angela Merkel

- Merrick Garland

- Tim Cook

- Antonin Scalia

Career Aptitude for Bureaucratic Assholes

Operations Manager / Compliance Officer: obsessed with order

Accountant / Auditor: sees beauty in rules and rows

Government Authority / Policy Enforcer: thrives in structured ecosystems

Production Designer: Builds functional sets within strict timelines and budgets

Bureaucratic Asshole Archetypes in Literature and Film

Miranda Priestly in *The Devil Wears Prada*

Sheldon Cooper in *Big Bang Theory*

Dolores Umbridge in the *Harry Potter Series*

Leslie Knope in *Parks and Recreation*

Dwight Schrute in *The Office*

Best Entertainment for Bureaucratic Assholes

Games: Sim City/The Sims, Agricola, Risk, Magic the Gathering, Sudoku

Music: Marching band, swing, traditional jazz

Stories: Procedural dramas and crime fiction (*Law and Order*), workplace dramas or comedies (*The Office, Parks and Recreation*), 20th century period films

Exercise/sports: Pilates, triathlon training, pickleball and other league sports

Other Activities: Sorting for fun (scheduling, budgeting, organizing, decluttering/cleaning), planning travel routes, event or battle reenactments, meditations via checklist, HOA meetings

Cocktail, Beer, and Wine Pairings for Scheming Assholes

Cocktail: Gin & Tonic — balanced, structured, and historically correct. It's got rules, ratios, and a colonial backbone.

Beer: Kölsch — clean, organized, deeply procedural

Wine: Chianti Classico — traditional, rule-abiding, structured

Tips for Dealing with a Bureaucratic Asshole

Working Relationships: Respect the system and tradition. Follow the rules or at least pretend to. They feel safest when things are predictable.

Domestic Relationships: Bring order, not drama. If you want a change, present a process. They show love through consistency, not spontaneity.

Bureaucratic Asshole Phrases

An easy way to identify a Bureaucratic Asshole (other than having them take the quiz, which is the easiest) is when you hear them utter a phrase that reveals their intent. It is likely that someone saying one of these phrases has the Bureaucratic trait in their profile as either their primary or secondary personality.

That's not how we do things. By violating an unspoken policy, you have reduced your personal trust factor by 20%.

Let's run it through the proper channels. This is another way of saying "We're going to delay this request instead of risking doing something unregulated or spontaneous that could break the system."

Did you even read the guidelines? The Beaver has read them multiple times, and they are ready to weaponize them if you dare to respond to this question.

Triggers for Bureaucratic Assholes

The Beaver has emotional and situational triggers that can make them lose their composure, at least momentarily. The table below lists some common triggers, why they disturb them, and some ideas on how to calm their nerves during and after a triggering.

Trigger	Why it upsets them	How to ease their nerves
Breaking protocol	Intentionally breaking the process feels like chaos and disrespect	Explain changes or exceptions (in advance if possible) and involve them early in process modifications
Ambiguity or vagueness	A lack of clarity verbally or in writing may cause anxiety and trigger resistance	Use specific, definitive steps, and include the what-ifs, or task them to help define them
Skipping steps	Skipping steps threatens order and may lead to unpredictability	Acknowledge existing shortcuts, provide an improvement plan, ask for input, and accept the input
Being excluded from planning	Feels disrespectful because planning is a strength of theirs and you should know that	Invite their structural input, even for a small part of the plan
Disorganization	A lack of organization overwhelms them and can break trust	Help them create systems to regain order, even if it's a temporary solution

Love for Bureaucratic Assholes

Best Love Match: Stoic Asshole

Why it works: Bureaucratic and Stoic share a systematic love. They appreciate dependability, planning, emotional consistency, and a mutual refusal to talk about feelings (unless it's scheduled in advance).

Bonus Love Sparks: Shared calendars, sorting together, folding laundry in silence

Bureaucratic Asshole Relationship Dynamics

The table below lists potential collaborations and pitfalls for the Bureaucratic Asshole as they try to deal with each of the other assholes in the zodiac who are less organized.

Assholes	Relationship Dynamic	Areas of Risk	Bonding Opportunities
Vanishing Asshole (Fox)	Structure vs. inconsistency	Beaver frustrated with flakiness	Teaching Fox how to follow-through and making small victories.
Scheming Asshole (Octopus)	Loophole landmines	Procedural clashes	Strategic implementation duo
Sanctimonious Asshole (Owl)	Policy meets principle	Competitive stubbornness when moralities clash	Shared passion for governance
Boastful Asshole (Peacock)	Order infusion into performance	Ego overload	Theater of respectability
Cynical Asshole (Cat)	Systems vs. snark	Constant criticism	Bonding over system critiques and planning reforms
Analytical Asshole (Falcon)	Efficiency soulmates	Emotional detachment	Flawless process execution

Assholes	Relationship Dynamic	Areas of Risk	Bonding Opportunities
Dramatic Asshole (Cockatoo)	Rules get rewritten	Emotional burnout	Discipline fuels creativity
Martyr Asshole (Elephant)	Duty overdrive	Resentment builds	Purpose through precision
Stoic Asshole (Tortoise)	Steady structure	Risk of boredom	Shared silence, consistency, and predictability
Codependent Asshole (Golden Retriever)	Rules vs. reassurance	Smothering tension	Comfort in routine care
Jester Asshole (Chimpanzee)	Chaos and compliance	Rule-breaking anxiety	Laughter as regulation relief injects fun into process maintenance

Ideal Purpose and Life Journey for The Bureaucratic Asshole

The ultimate life purpose for a Bureaucratic Asshole is in the creation and adherence to a system that serves the common good. They apply their devotion to structure and talent for problem solving not for personal gain or ideological status, but for a humanitarian cause that gets attention.

Along the way they will gain momentum and insight by learning how to recognize their own OCD triggers and the triggers of others for the purpose of making communicating easier with the weaker, messier architypes. They may spend time in communities who lack more modern conveniences, technologies, or systems and begin to problem solve for them on a budget to help them find the virtue and efficiency in implementing order.

Their successful journey begins as a rigid rule follower whose instinct is to critique systemic flaws, and color code people and ideas into proper categories for ease of definition and recall (many people find this practice intimidating and authoritative). In the end, their altruistic efforts inventing a manageable solution designed with empathy, care and purpose lead to a legendary reputation that the beneficiaries of the system remember with affection.

"I love people. I just can't stand being around them for long."

— Charles Bukowski

The Vanishing Asshole

Animal Spirit: Fox

Motivational Driver: Avoidance

Best Traits: Independent, elusive

Worst Traits: Non-committal, manipulative through absence

Vanishing Asshole Profile

You are mysterious, self-contained, and endlessly adaptive. You're the master of knowing when to appear and when to vanish. Your independence is inspiring. Your detachment is intriguing. People are fascinated by your unpredictability and drawn to your elusive charm.

You give just enough to stay in the game but never so much that you lose yourself. You observe, say little, and act with precision. People long to understand you. Some might call you withdrawn or aloof, but really you're just too evolved to waste time on things that don't serve you. You're not absent — you're selective. Your quiet exits and reappearances are tactical. You are the ghost in the machine, the whisper behind the curtain. You control the narrative and your own fate by staying unreadable. You are a sharp and deep silence in a world that overshares.

Famous Vanishing Assholes

The Ghost: Elusive, independent, disappears at will

- The Artist (formerly known as Prince)
- J.D. Salinger
- Lauryn Hill
- Bill Watterson
- David Bowie

Career Aptitude for Vanishing Assholes

Private Investigator / Intelligence Analyst: works in shadows, sees all

Solo Artist / Writer: creates on their own terms

Digital Nomad / Project Consultant: all-in for the moment then disappears when it gets claustrophobic

Vanishing Asshole Archetypes in Literature and Film

Clementine Kruczynski in *Eternal Sunshine of the Spotless Mind*

Frank Abagnale Jr. in *Catch Me If You Can*

Howl in *Howl's Moving Castle*

Reese Bobby in *Talladega Nights*

Charlie Cale in *Poker Face*

Best Entertainment for Vanishing Assholes

Games: Sim Games, Minecraft, Return of the Obra Dinn, Outer Wilds

Music: Experimental (Frank Zappa, Brian Eno), alternative rock, dream pop, ambient folk music (Emma Ruth Rundle)

Stories: Mysteries, philosophical novels, Neo-noir (Blade Runner, Fargo, Memento), Art House films

Exercise/sports: Trail walking/running, climbing, night swimming, solo yoga

Other Activities: Unmapped walks (especially in new places), people watching, isolation tanks, a secret craft performed quietly and obsessively with no external validation needed.

Cocktail, Beer, and Wine Pairings for Vanishing Assholes

Cocktail: Corpse Reviver No. 2 — mysterious, forgotten, and low-key magical. Shows up, haunts you, disappears again.

Beer: Saison — ephemeral, funky, unpredictable

Wine: Orange Wine — obscure, intriguing, never fully understood

Tips for Dealing with a Vanishing Asshole

Working Relationships: Don't chase or corner them, because they'll vanish again. Offer flexibility and indirect support. Keep check-ins chill, not intense.

Domestic Relationships: Create safe, low-pressure spaces. They'll return when it feels easy to exist around you. Don't guilt-trip their absence.

Vanishing Asshole Phrases

An easy way to identify a Vanishing Asshole (other than having them take the quiz, which is the easiest) is when you hear them utter a phrase that reveals their intent. It is likely that someone saying one of these phrases has the Vanishing trait in their profile as either their primary or secondary personality.

OK, let me get back to you on that. They won't. But this answer buys some time to disappear without confrontation.

I've just had a lot going on lately...so busy. You have been ghosted but here's a vague apology in exchange for not digging deeper.

I believe people come into your life for a reason. Seems like that reason with us is about over. I'm already emotionally packed and halfway out the door.

Triggers for Vanishing Assholes

The Fox has emotional and situational triggers that can make them lose their composure, at least momentarily. The table below lists some common triggers and some ideas on how to calm their nerves during and after a triggering.

Trigger	Why it upsets them	How to ease their nerves
Emotional confrontation	Loud emotions feel threatening. The Fox will seek to escape	Use a low-pressure tone and speak indirectly about issues
Too many demands	A long list of demands is overwhelming and can be impossible to digest	Space requests out over time
Loss of autonomy	A Fox without independence is suffocating	Frame commitments as optional and flexible to at least give them the illusion of autonomy
Being "seen"	Someone who exposes their propensity to avoidance is someone to avoid	Validate their feelings without pressing them on their nature
Over-attentive behavior from others	Giving them too much attention over several days may trigger withdrawal	Give them some breathing room between engagements

Love for Vanishing Assholes

Best Love Match: Cynical Asshole

Why it works: No one gets suffocated. No one over-promises. Both Vanishing and Cynical respect independence and keep things light until trust naturally builds. They give each other space. They share an appreciation for music, literature, design, and mood lighting. They also share a fondness for inside jokes, quiet rebellion, and a mutual refusal to be owned by the world.

Bonus Love Sparks: They flirt through shared eye rolls and deadpan takes. The world's absurdity is their aphrodisiac. They blow off events together and happily stay at home. Laughter, especially the dark and dry kind, becomes foreplay.

Vanishing Asshole Relationship Dynamics

The table below lists potential collaborations and pitfalls for the Vanishing Asshole as they deal with each of the other assholes in the zodiac.

Assholes	Relationship Dynamic	Areas of Risk	Bonding Opportunities
Scheming Asshole (Octopus)	Strategic ghosting	Emotional unavailability	Covert alliance
Sanctimonious Asshole (Owl)	Morality press	Fox evades judgment	Shared exposure of corruption
Boastful Asshole (Peacock)	Mystery pokes vanity	Disappearing act triggers Peacock insecurity	Romantic tension, elusive charm
Cynical Asshole (Cat)	Mutual avoidance of all the crap	Emotional apathy	Silent companionship
Analytical Asshole (Falcon)	Plan meets unpredictability	Fox resists over-analysis	Curiosity and intrigue
Dramatic Asshole (Cockatoo)	Intensity vs. evasion	Fox avoids emotional explosions	The magnetism of mystery

Assholes	Relationship Dynamic	Areas of Risk	Bonding Opportunities
Martyr Asshole (Elephant)	Abandonment sorrows	Guilt trip triggers vanishing	Moments of forgiveness and redemption
Stoic Asshole (Tortoise)	Parallel detachment	Little to no engagement	Safe zones with low-pressure trust
Codependent Asshole (Golden Retriever)	Escaping the cling	Devastating disconnection	Occasional soft landings
Jester Asshole (Chimpanzee)	Hide and seek	Chaos limits trust	Playful, erratic spark
Bureaucratic Asshole (Beaver)	Schedule meets smoke bomb	Beaver frustrated with flakiness	Teaching Fox how to follow-through

Ideal Purpose and Life Journey for The Vanishing Asshole

The ultimate life purpose for a Vanishing Asshole is to show others how purposeful non-attachment can be a positive path to inner peace, clarity, and quiet rebellion.

Along the way they will gain momentum and insight by honing their observation and comprehension skills, which encourages their confidence and selective participation, and by identifying role models who do-good-and-disappear. They discover that while severe detachment prevents pain, it also prevents joy, and so they strive to maintain a measured balance between being an introvert and putting themselves out into the world. They may perform works or deeds anonymously to get their message out without drawing attention to their personal life.

Their successful journey begins as someone whose instinct for detachment and ghosting others is based on self-preservation. As they mature and become anchored, their vanishing act evolves as a part of a creative independence that serves to maximize their impact when they are present and sharing their knowledge or talent. Instead of withdrawing out of fear, they now withdraw to gain clarity, then return with significant insight or action, or not at all. Their life reveals a wisdom of impermanence and self-sovereignty that inspires others to be more confident and empowered. They are a role model for a lightness and satisfaction that comes with not drawing attention to one's own accomplishments or good deeds.

Appendix A: The Quiz

"My husband designed a personality test.
Turns out I'm a Scheming Asshole. Funny how that works."

— Karen Hayes

The following questions determine your asshole profile with primary and secondary traits. You can also take the quiz online at **https://www.assholezodiac.com**

If you intend to take the quiz more than once, write down your answers on a separate piece of paper for scoring. First, mark the checkboxes (only one box per question) or write down the numbers and letters of your corresponding answers separately. The scoring rationale appears after the initial quiz questions below.

After finishing question #5, you will be asked to score your primary motivational driver, which determines the group that you should proceed to for answering question #6. Questions 7, 8, and 9 do not rely on your motivational driver.

For each question, select only one best answer.

Question 1. In a conflict, your instinct is to....

☐ 1A   Stand up for what is right, no matter the cost

☐ 1B   Find a way to win or be admired

☐ 1C   Control the situation and find a solution

☐ 1D   Avoid the drama and protect my peace

Question 2. What motivates you the most?

☐ 2A Being a good person and doing the right thing

☐ 2B Standing out and being appreciated

☐ 2C Having things under control and being effective

☐ 2D Avoiding pain and discomfort

Question 3. What is your biggest fear?

☐ 3A Being unethical or immoral

☐ 3B Being ignored or insignificant

☐ 3C Being powerless or chaotic

☐ 3D Being trapped in obligations or in pain

Question 4. Which description fits you best?

☐ 4A   Principled and righteous

☐ 4B   Expressive and admired

☐ 4C   Organized and dependable

☐ 4D   Free spirited and elusive

Question 5. How do you get what you want?

☐ 5A   By appealing to principles and a higher purpose

☐ 5B   By being impressive and charismatic

☐ 5C   By taking charge and solving problems

☐ 5D   By staying out of the way and letting things happen

Scoring Part 1. Use hashmarks on the scoring table below in accordance with your answers for questions 1-5. Which letter had the most answers (A, B, C, or D)?

	A	B	C	D
Question 1				
Question 2				
Question 3				
Question 4				
Question 5				
Total				

Move to one of the question #6 options below. Answer the #6 question that corresponds to your highest scoring letter out of the first 5 questions, i.e., if you had the most answers under A, go to question 6A and skip questions 6B, 6C, and 6D.

In the rare occasion your answers for questions #1 through #5 result in a tie of 2 points each for A,B,C, or D, then answer each of the Question #6 subsections that correspond to those two letters. For instance, if you answered twice with A answers and twice with C answers, then move on to answer both Question 6A and 6C below.

Question 6A. How do you typically uphold your moral convictions?

☐ 6A.1   Through strategy and behind-the-scenes influence

☐ 6A.2   Through vocal integrity and taking the high road

☐ 6A.3   Through enforcing rules and keeping systems fair

Question 6B. How do you seek recognition from others?

☐ 6B.1   By impressing them with my image and success

☐ 6B.2   By sharing emotional truth and vulnerability

☐ 6B.3   By using wit, humor, and cleverness to win attention

Question 6C. How do you maintain your sense of control?

☐ 6C.1   By analyzing everything and cutting to the truth

☐ 6C.2   By over-functioning and taking responsibility for others

☐ 6C.3   By staying emotionally reserved and unflappable

Question 6D. When things get emotionally complex, what's your default?

☐ 6D.1   I detach and turn to sarcasm or dark humor

☐ 6D.2   I overinvest in others emotionally to stay close

☐ 6D.3   I pull away completely and disappear for a while

Scoring Part 2. Check your answer to question 6 on the table below to reveal your primary asshole personality type. The answer to Question #6 is worth 3 points in your total score. Then move on to Question #7 through #9 to see if you have any secondary traits.

If your answer to Question 6 was...	Then your Primary Asshole Type is...	Point Value
6A1	Scheming (Octopus)	(3 points)
6A2	Sanctimonious (Owl)	(3 points)
6A3	Bureaucratic (Beaver)	(3 points)
6B1	Boastful (Peacock)	(3 points)
6B2	Dramatic (Cockatoo)	(3 points)
6B3	Jester (Chimpanzee)	(3 points)
6C1	Analytical (Falcon)	(3 points)
6C2	Martyr (Elephant)	(3 points)
6C3	Stoic (Tortoise)	(3 points)
6D1	Cynical (Cat)	(3 points)
6D2	Codependent (Golden Retriever)	(3 points)
6D3	Vanishing (Fox)	(3 points)
Total		

Question 7. Select the one answer that best describes how you want others to experience you.

☐ 7.1   Strategic and in control of everything

☐ 7.2   Deeply moral and principled

☐ 7.3   Reliable and organized

☐ 7.4   Charming and impressive

☐ 7.5   Emotionally gripping and memorable

☐ 7.6   Witty and sharp

☐ 7.7   Logical and honest

☐ 7.8   Hardworking and selfless

☐ 7.9   Calm and unshakeable

☐ 7.10   Detached and sarcastic

☐ 7.11   Caring and emotionally available

☐ 7.12   Mysterious and independent

Question 8. Select the one response that best describes how you behave under stress.

☐ 8.1   I quietly strategize and try to control all outcomes

☐ 8.2   I call out what is wrong and take a moral stand

☐ 8.3   I take charge and get things back in order

☐ 8.4   I show off and over-perform to feel valuable

☐ 8.5   I express strong emotions and break down

☐ 8.6   I make jokes or deflect with humor

☐ 8.7   I analyze everything and retreat emotionally

☐ 8.8   I over-function and try to help everyone

☐ 8.9   I stay calm and shut down emotionally

☐ 8.10   I withdraw and become cynical

☐ 8.11   I over-nurture and stay glued to others

☐ 8.12   I try to escape or emotionally disappear

Question 9. Select the one answer that best describes your ideal environment.

☐ 9.1   A world I can quietly control

☐ 9.2   A principled place with shared values

☐ 9.3   A structured, well-run system

☐ 9.4   A stage where I shine

☐ 9.5   An emotionally expressive and connected place

☐ 9.6   A fast, witty, and energetic atmosphere

☐ 9.7   An efficient place where logic rules

☐ 9.8   A place where I am needed and appreciated

☐ 9.9   A calm, quiet zone without drama

☐ 9.10   An ironic world where no one takes it seriously

☐ 9.11   A warm, emotionally available environment

☐ 9.12   A place where I can disappear and reappear freely

Scoring Part 3. Complete Score. On the following table, enter your primary personality assigned from Question #6, worth 3 points (if you had a tied score enter both as primary for 3 points each). Then enter one point for each personality category scored from questions #7-9 as shown.

	Enter Primary Profile Assignment from Question #6	**Score**
Primary Asshole Personality		**3**
Other primary (if applicable)		
Answers from questions 7, 8, and 9	**Secondary Traits**	**Score**
7.1, 8.1, 9.1	Scheming (Octopus)	
7.2, 8.2, 9.2	Sanctimonious (Owl)	
7.3, 8.3, 9.3	Bureaucratic (Beaver)	
7.4, 8.4, 9.4	Boastful (Peacock)	
7.5, 8.5, 9.5	Dramatic (Cockatoo)	
7.6, 8.6, 9.6	Jester (Chimpanzee)	
7.7, 8.7, 9.7	Analytical (Falcon)	
7.8, 8.8, 9.8	Martyr (Elephant)	
7.9, 8.9, 9.9	Stoic (Tortoise)	
7.10, 8.10, 9.10	Cynical (Cat)	
7.11, 8.11, 9.11	Codependent (Golden Retriever)	
7.12, 8.12, 9.12	Vanishing (Fox)	

If you had a tied primary persona for question #6 (two categories that each scored 2 points in questions #1-5, and one other lone outlier category), your answers from #7-9 may break the tie to determine your Primary Asshole Type with a Strong Secondary as the other.

Most people will score some secondary personality traits. If you take the quiz at different times, you may see a strong secondary become your primary profile (depending on your mood, or what type of assholes you are sharing space with when you take the quiz). See Appendix C for more information about Secondaries.

Appendix B: Motivational Drivers

Each asshole personality type in the Asshole Zodiac operates from one of four deep-rooted motivational drivers. These are the primary emotional engines behind their behavior, affecting probable blind spots, and fueling personal justifications. An understanding of the relevant motivational drivers helps interpret why an asshole acts the way they do, especially when they are being difficult.

The motivational drivers are color coded in the zodiac wheel shown on the cover of this book: Moral Enforcement (red), Performance (blue), Avoidance (green), and Control (orange).

Moral Enforcement

The core desire of a personality type driven by Moral Enforcement is to uphold a personal or ideological vision of right and wrong. These assholes believe they have a duty to correct, convert, or outlast the wrongness of others. The exact flavor of their belief and behavior varies a bit for the three related asshole types:

The Scheming Asshole: Morality for the Octopus is not necessarily based on any particular religion or societal norm. They have their own personal morality, which is the correct one. When critiquing the correctness of people and systems, Scheming Assholes can be seen as having a superiority complex, which they know is a thing. That's why they often deliver measured responses to selective audiences. They make backup plans that will further their goals, anticipating conflict with other assholes. The Schemer gets people to follow their rules using strategy as opposed to preaching, and unlike other types, their morality is subject to change under the right conditions. Not that they were ever wrong — lessons are a part of their journey.

The Sanctimonious Asshole: The Owl has a strong internal sense of right and wrong, providing an unshakable foundation that translates easily to politics, religion, lifestyle, or etiquette. They truly think it's their moral obligation to point out the moral faults in others for the greater good and they are happy to lend their advice as mentors in any setting. They will sacrifice being liked for being right. Grey areas of morality are uncomfortable for them, and they will put in substantial effort to sort the greys into palatable blacks and whites.

The Bureaucratic Asshole: The Beaver comes across as judgy with quick reprimands and corrections, but it's not personal. Their moral driver is more about process than people and they assume you don't have the capacity to fully understand your error. They are glad to help you fix a problem and might even fix it for you right now while you're talking about it with a "just let me do it" shove, because it's just going to take too long to explain the intricacies of moral truth to a non-bureaucrat. Even if you do wind up understanding the issue, that doesn't mean you're going to do the right thing any time soon, so step aside.

Performance

The core desire of a personality type driven by Performance is to be seen, appreciated, and admired. These assholes need an audience. They daydream of having recognition and veer into performative behavior whenever they need a fix. The exact flavor of their performative behavior varies a bit for the three related asshole types:

The Boastful Asshole: The Peacock knows that admiration is fleeting if you don't nurture it. It's not only vanity at work here; there's a deep healing gain when receiving recognition, which is critical to maintaining their self-worth and to stay productive. You may find them dominating conversations, name-dropping, or humble-bragging under a veil of self-deprecation, in service of staying at center stage. If their bravado doesn't yield a positive result, they'll take the negative to tide them over until you all can see the light. You'll already be looking when it comes.

The Dramatic Asshole: The Cockatoo doesn't only want to be seen; they need to be *felt*. Their performance is addressed to your very soul to illicit joy and heartbreak on both primal and spiritual levels. Their speeches are inspiring. Their outbursts are exhausting. Using emotional expressiveness, high-stakes storytelling, and a flair for exaggeration, this bird performs to ensure it captures your attention by being the most dazzling in the room, or the most wounded, or preferably both.

The Jester Asshole: The Chimpanzee feeds on laughter, gasps, and chortles. They need someone to appreciate their humor. Just one kid in the classroom is enough to validate their snark even if everyone else is against them. They perform comedy as a weapon to deflect vulnerability, disarm the tension in the room, and sidestep sincerity when it becomes too awkward for them. The alternative is being boring, invisible, or dismissed, which are all unbearable outcomes.

Avoidance

The core desire of a personality type driven by Avoidance is to feel emotionally safe. They have a need for connection and human bonding absent of conflict. These assholes may overpromise, over give, and under-assert in an effort to please others and maintain a close relationship. They seek harmony, sometimes at their own expense, and are willing to go to extremes to get it. Removing themselves from stressful situations is common, but the exact flavor of their behavior varies a bit for the three related asshole types:

The Codependent Asshole: The Golden Retriever's emotional landscape is ruled by the dread of possible abandonment, and they will twist themselves into knots to stay needed, wanted, and useful. Their first instinct is to avoid conflict, or any topic that might disrupt their own sense of value in a relationship, but when conflict appears to be unavoidable their compassion and support can quickly switch to disfunction-as-punishment with a demand for appreciation. Underneath it all, they just want someone to look them in the eye and say, "You're enough — even if you stop doing everything."

The Cynical Asshole: The Cat is a master of avoidance as a survival tactic with their reflexive rejections of connections and controls. They are always prepared to declare sincere connections unattainable and label controls as bullshit. Vulnerability feels like danger, so their apathy is a worthy armor. Emotionally withdrawn and intellectually sharp, they keep others at arm's length using brilliant strokes of sarcasm, skepticism, and outright dismissal. It's not that they inherently distrust all people; they distrust hope, sincerity, systems, and sometimes even themselves.

The Vanishing Asshole: The Fox does want to connect with others but on their own unpredictable terms. They despise vulnerability and the dependencies that come with it, so they avoid social bondage by vanishing regularly. They often live in a push-pull cycle: appearing warm, witty, and intriguing just long enough to earn trust, and then disappearing before they can be truly known. They tend to be creative, introspective, observant, and uniquely empathetic, preferring to shine for a while, then escape to recover. What they need most is permission to return without punishment whenever they're ready to leave their hole.

Control

The core desire of a personality type driven by Control is to live in a predictable world where chaos can be lassoed or dampened with minimal impact to their environment. To this end, they may micromanage, preempt disruption, or establish routines to limit randomness. They create rules, either for themselves or others, to maintain the vibration that makes sense to them and that they require to function properly without distractions. The exact flavor of their behavior varies a bit for the three related asshole types:

Analytical Asshole: The Falcon's lust for control is driven by their need for understanding. Their clarity prevents chaos. They don't just want answers — they need those answers to make sense. Order, logic, data, and structure are their emotional support systems, and anything unpredictable is treated as a threat to be neutralized, lest they be exposed as fallible. They assert control not with authority, but with scientific research and a course correction that allows them to breathe.

Stoic Asshole: The Tortoise exerts control through emotional restraint. For them, remaining calm is a defense mechanism that protects them and others from instability. They resist emotional demands and see vulnerability as a potential liability. Their stillness is discipline, not apathy. Predictability is their goal. They make contingency plans so that there is no surprise that catches their psyche off guard. Their internal version of control means keeping themselves measured and rational, especially when others can't seem to. They will manage discomfort by withdrawing, minimizing potential impact, or by intellectualizing it away. If they can master themselves, they can survive whatever the world throws their way.

Martyr Asshole: The Elephant controls the herd through strategic self-sacrifice and by using guilt as leverage. Their instinct for control comes from a basic belief that if they don't hold everything together, no one else will. Their loyalty, bravery, competence, and commitment to service are legendary, but their favors and suffering become a measurable currency. They don't fear the hard work — they fear irrelevance and encroaching mayhem when others don't notice, reciprocate, or validate their efforts. Make sure they are well appreciated, because betrayal is a theft of that currency, and it triggers an elephant-sized grudge.

Appendix C: Secondary Profiles

It is rare that someone will match a particular asshole profile at 100%.

Most people will have one or more secondary traits that influence their behavior. Sometimes those secondary asshole types share the same motivational drivers. The fun part is when the secondaries have different motivational drivers. That's when personalities can become colorful, complex, and really interesting.

A secondary asshole trait can explain unexpected remarks and behaviors from a person you think you know. When you urge someone to show their genuine personality because they seem too reserved, they may just switch to their strongest secondary personae because you seem to like it better. People who have a mastery of their asshole personas and can switch at will have a strong social advantage by being able to perform to the audience at hand. Most of us, however, are at the mercy of our mood, stress levels, and things that trigger our alternate traits.

A Stoic Asshole is going to seem calm and unbothered most of the time. If their secondary is a Jester or Dramatic Asshole, you might be alarmed when they begin to perform with a non-characteristic absurdity or an emotionally compelling monologue.

A Boastful Asshole with an Analytic secondary might have moments of divine persuasion as they present what you thought was a petty argument using enough logic and data to turn the debate.

A Codependent Asshole with a Martyr secondary can spin you quickly into a guilt trip about a subject that you always assumed had their full support.

A Cynical Asshole with a Bureaucratic secondary may stridently defend the same process that you have already heard them besmirch and denigrate.

These variables can easily confuse our perception of the people we're around regularly and even put us off balance. Some display their personas situationally, like using their primary at work and their secondary at home or at play, or when discussing a certain topic like politics or religion. But if you know their complete profile, it all makes sense; the less you'll be surprised at their behavior modes, and the more you'll be able to anticipate their sudden personality pops. When you're aware of your own complete Asshole profile, you can easily sort out your behavioral motivations and identify which persona is driving you, when, with whom, and under what circumstance. It's a simple and powerful introspection tool.

Appendix D:
Notes about your asshole friends

Use the following worksheet to make your best guess about what type of asshole represents your friends, family, or colleagues. When the time is right, have them take the quiz at **https://www.assholezodiac.com/the-quiz.html** or conduct it and score it yourself using the questions in Appendix A: The Quiz.

Name	Asshole Type Guess	Actual Asshole Type
_____	_____	_____
_____	_____	_____
_____	_____	_____
_____	_____	_____
_____	_____	_____
_____	_____	_____
_____	_____	_____
_____	_____	_____
_____	_____	_____
_____	_____	_____
_____	_____	_____
_____	_____	_____
_____	_____	_____
_____	_____	_____
_____	_____	_____

About the Authors

Todd and Karen Hayes are assholes living in Texas.